AMERICA'S NUCLEAR
CROSSROADS

A FORWARD-LOOKING ANTHOLOGY

EDITED BY
CAROLINE DORMINEY
AND ERIC GOMEZ

CATO
INSTITUTE

Copyright © 2019 by the Cato Institute.
All rights reserved.

Print ISBN: 978-1-948647-70-0
eBook ISBN: 978-1-948647-71-7

Library of Congress Cataloging-in-Publication Data available.

Cover design: Jon Meyers

Printed in the United States of America.

CATO INSTITUTE
1000 Massachusetts Avenue, NW
Washington, DC 20001
www.cato.org

Contents

Foreword

Janne E. Nolan

After more than a decade spent grappling with the challenges of irregular warfare and violent extremism, the U.S. national security community has largely shifted its collective attention to interstate power politics. Nuclear weapons figure prominently in this new reality. The 2018 *Nuclear Posture Review* prompted Americans to contemplate the use of nuclear weapons by either the United States or its potential adversaries in a future conflict in Europe or Asia. Even before the Trump administration gave voice to this shift, the United States had already embarked on a costly, long-delayed modernization of major elements of its nuclear arsenal. All three legs of the "triad" of land-based intercontinental ballistic missiles, nuclear-armed manned aircraft, and submarine-launched ballistic missiles will be updated.

According to some observers, these developments reflect the emergence of a new Cold War. For others, the challenge is not how best to engage in "strategic competition," but how to avoid backsliding into outmoded analogies and concepts. As with any debate, there are elements of truth on both sides. Russia and China have both shown themselves to have regional aspirations, and possibly global ambitions, that are at odds with the aims of U.S. foreign policy. Russia's annexation of Crimea was a turning point for many analysts within the U.S. national security community, demonstrating the Putin regime's willingness to engage in the almost antiquated practice of territorial conquest. In the Asia-Pacific region, China's aggressiveness in its maritime periphery has frustrated the efforts of successive U.S. presidential administrations to integrate China into a U.S.-led economic and political order.

On the other hand, many of the analytical concepts and policy tools that served the United States well during the Cold War seem vastly ill-equipped for the present moment. The challenge posed by Russia largely stems not from its military and economic might, but from its conventional military weakness and economic stagnation. China is also not the Soviet Union. U.S.-China relations take place in a radically different geographic, political, and economic context. China's nuclear forces are also significantly smaller than the Soviet Union's, and China depends less on its nuclear arsenal to deter conventional military escalation.

The ongoing modernization program for U.S. nuclear forces also hearkens back to an earlier time. The previous and current modernization programs both had their genesis under Democratic presidents but were accelerated under their Republican successors. The similarities end there. The last time the United States embarked on a major modernization of its nuclear forces, under President Jimmy Carter, the Soviet Union and the United States both maintained an active stockpile of tens of thousands of nuclear-armed missiles and bombs, of which thousands were maintained on 24-hour alert. Today, far fewer U.S. and Russian weapons are on alert, and since 1991 the United States has dramatically reduced its arsenal of so-called tactical nuclear weapons, even eliminating entire classes of weapons.[1]

More importantly, the modernization effort begun by Carter and continued by President Ronald Reagan took place in a fundamentally different political context. That era was defined by robust bipartisan consensus on the roles assigned to nuclear weapons as well as the necessity of balancing deterrence and modernization with diplomacy. Today's congressional Republicans and Democrats continue to broadly agree on the importance of modernizing U.S. nuclear forces and the complex of facilities that supports them. And both parties agree in broad terms that Russia and China pose unique military and political challenges to the security of the United States and its allies. But gone is political consensus on the security-enhancing benefits of situating U.S. nuclear force posture within a verifiable, pragmatic diplomatic framework.

During the Cold War, a broad swath of leaders in both parties recognized the essential and inherent synergies between fielding credible deterrent forces and taking pragmatic steps to reduce the risks of nuclear competition. Today, activists in both parties are thoroughly challenging this consensus. Upstart voices on both the left and right seem increasingly skeptical that long-term force planning and sustained engagement on nuclear risk reduction are mutually reinforcing. Yet military leaders assert this very fact: it is vastly easier for the United States to procure and posture forces if adversary forces are constrained and routinely monitored.[2] If this consensus continues to fray, the United States may find itself facing a vastly changed strategic landscape without the modicum of stability gained from having regular insight into Russia's nuclear forces through ongoing treaty verification.

Perhaps the most troubling difference between the Cold War and the present moment is the yawning gap between the priorities and perceptions of analysts and decisionmakers and those of the broader American public. According to a 2017 poll by the Chicago Council on Global Affairs, a majority of Americans do not support the use of American troops to defend U.S. allies in a hypothetical conflict with Russia or China.[3] No major polls have been conducted on public attitudes toward nuclear modernization, but a 2018 Gallup survey found that almost two-thirds of Americans believe that defense spending is about right or too high.[4] It remains to be seen whether this rare area of bipartisan agreement can withstand the politicization that pervades almost every other area of national policy. Today, leaders have done little to prepare their constituents for a return to "great power competition," while steadily increasing the burdens imposed on the few Americans who wear the uniform.

Even this cursory review of the historical record highlights the challenge facing future strategists, scholars, and analysts. On the one hand, many of the current generation of practitioners and thinkers seem to have lost sight of the lessons of the Cold War. On the other hand, today's nuclear challenges are manifestly different and more complex, demanding new frameworks and novel ways to apply the lessons of the past. This volume addresses those lapses and the challenges ahead.

The contributors to this volume question and potentially recast some of the fundamental assumptions underlying both the theory and practice of nuclear deterrence. Each chapter challenges some element of the conventional wisdom and makes the case for a fresh look at how the

United States leverages its nuclear and nonnuclear military assets to deter aggression against itself and its allies and partners. The volume also raises questions pertaining to some challenges, such as new technologies and new players, that lack clear historical parallels. Equally striking is the diversity of professional backgrounds and perspectives among the contributors, who represent the next generation of scholars and practitioners. While no consensus can emerge from such a diverse group of thinkers, every contributor engages in a refreshing and rigorous interrogation of tough questions, with a firm grounding in the latest research and historically informed analysis.

Note from the Editors: Janne E. Nolan passed away shortly before this volume went to press—we are deeply grateful for her contribution. Janne was a pillar of this community who made significant contributions to the field of nuclear policy; her tireless mentorship helped many emerging experts. She enriched the lives of those who knew her. Janne will be dearly missed.

Introduction

Caroline Dorminey and Eric Gomez

After nearly three decades of effectively unrivaled U.S. dominance of the international system, a renewed focus on great power competition is coinciding with a fraying of old arms control agreements and a major U.S. nuclear modernization effort. Policy issues in nuclear deterrence and arms control are poised to return to a level of importance in U.S. national security strategy not seen since the end of the Cold War. Furthermore, the policy solutions that Washington crafts over the next few years will heavily influence U.S. nuclear strategy for decades to come.

As policymakers think about what solutions to apply to new nuclear challenges, they will likely look to the Cold War for guidance. Examining the last time that the United States had to contend with a nuclear-armed, great power adversary—a time that also produced a wealth of theoretical and practical knowledge on nuclear policy issues—is an entirely sensible course of action. However, looking too closely to the past for answers to contemporary challenges also carries risk. Changing political, technical, and strategic factors make for policy problems that don't always neatly align with Cold War conditions and, by extension, Cold War solutions. Gen. John Hyten, commander of U.S. Strategic Command, put it this way in February 2018: "The [nuclear] doctrine we came up with 50 years ago is still valid but *it is not current*. And so, we have to move into currency and we have to think about how the world is different and what should we do that's different."[1] The theories and policies that may have served the United States well during the Cold War are valuable for thinking through contemporary problems, but they may not always offer the best solutions for new challenges.

America's Nuclear Crossroads: A Forward-Looking Anthology brings together a group of diverse thinkers from government, think tanks, and academia to examine nine nuclear puzzles that American policymakers are trying to solve. The primary focus of the anthology is to lay out actionable recommendations for policymakers grappling with nuclear deterrence and arms control challenges. While each chapter is rooted in a broader historical or academic understanding of the issue it examines, the history and theory are distilled and used as a framework for understanding challenges and the proposed solutions. *America's Nuclear Crossroads* examines the nuclear policy problems of today with an eye toward the future, not the past.

The nine chapters of the anthology are roughly divided into three categories: domestic-facing U.S. nuclear policy issues, such as the modernization budget; international-facing nuclear deterrence challenges, including the U.S.-Russia and U.S.-China nuclear relationships; and the future of arms control.

The first three chapters examine defense-focused policy problems that impact the structure and future of American capabilities. Chapter 1, by Caroline Dorminey, analyzes the United States' $1 trillion-plus nuclear modernization plan with a critical eye for how different priorities could clash with one another as different weapons programs move through the development cycle. She also sets forth multiple options for adjusting the nuclear modernization plan with an emphasis on long-term cost savings. The second chapter, written by Eric Gomez, focuses on U.S. missile defense capabilities and the impact these systems have on nuclear stability. Chapter 2 explains why wholesale U.S. missile defense expansion will have negative implications for nuclear stability, and it argues for expanding regional systems while limiting homeland defense systems to mitigate the destabilizing consequences. Chapter 3, by Todd Harrison, outlines the challenges to nuclear deterrence created by the second space age and proposes ways to reduce the vulnerabilities of contemporary U.S. space-based systems to improve nuclear stability.

Chapters 4 through 7 examine nuclear challenges in America's foreign policy. Chapter 4, written by Olga Oliker, explores the assumptions and beliefs undergirding the U.S.-Russia nuclear relationship and shows how each country's perception of the other is contributing to an erosion of deterrence and decreasing nuclear stability.

The next two chapters both discuss U.S. extended deterrence commitments but arrive at different policy recommendations. Austin Long's Chapter 5 lays out the costs and benefits of a damage-limitation strategy toward China and concludes that this more competitive nuclear posture could have significant benefits for extended deterrence despite its attendant increase in escalation risks. In contrast, Eric Gomez's Chapter 6 questions the credibility of U.S. nuclear threats for deterring the most likely forms of great power conflict. The chapter goes on to argue that nonnuclear capabilities may be better suited for both deterring these conflicts and controlling escalation should deterrence fail.

Chapter 7, by Matthew Fuhrmann and Todd S. Sechser, is a distillation of their book *Nuclear Weapons and Coercive Diplomacy* and addresses the threat of rogue states like Iran and North Korea using nuclear weapons to coerce other countries. Their chapter shows that while states may try to use nuclear weapons for coercion, such efforts rarely succeed. Therefore, the threat of nuclear blackmail is manageable and does not warrant the use of military force to disarm rogue states before they can develop a nuclear arsenal.

Chapters 8 and 9 deal with the future of arms control, from both the American and international perspectives. Maggie Tennis's Chapter 8 examines U.S. arms control efforts under the Trump administration, which can best be described as a wrecking ball. She argues that U.S. policymakers should focus their efforts on extending New START (the 2010 iteration of the Strategic Arms Reduction Treaty) given the treaty's clear benefits and to keep the United States involved in arms control despite the administration's decisions to leave or destroy other agreements. Finally, Beatrice Fihn's Chapter 9 explains the history and motivations of the nuclear ban movement, which spearheaded an effort to create a new international treaty outlawing nuclear weapons. Understanding and engaging with the arguments raised by the ban movement will likely become more important for U.S. policymakers as the ban treaty gains more support.

We compiled *America's Nuclear Crossroads* to serve as a reference tool for policymakers and laypeople alike as they navigate an increasingly complex nuclear security environment. The debates and policy decisions that play out over the next few years will likely affect America's nuclear deterrence and arms control strategies for decades to come and be the opening move in a new era of great power competition. This anthology offers a wide view of the most pressing nuclear challenges the United States is facing at this crossroads. While one anthology cannot resolve every emerging problem, we hope that these chapters spark a broader dialogue and offer some initial policy recommendations for solving said challenges.

1. Buying the Bang for Fewer Bucks
Managing Nuclear Modernization Costs
Caroline Dorminey

Creating, deploying, and maintaining the American nuclear arsenal is an extremely costly, but necessary, enterprise. This chapter explores options for reducing the costs of the ongoing nuclear modernization plan not only for the sake of cost savings, but also because of strategic utility. There are ample opportunities to craft a revised nuclear modernization plan that better reflects the shifting strategic priorities and the evolution of threats facing the United States.

Most of the nation's current nuclear forces—both delivery platforms and warheads—are nearing the end of their service lives. Naturally, the time has come to make decisions on how to either extend those service lives through Life Extension Programs (LEPs) or replace the systems entirely with upgrades.

Over the next 30 years, the U.S. military plans to either replace or expand the number of platforms with the aim to reach 12 nuclear ballistic missile submarines (SSBNs), 400 fielded intercontinental ballistic missiles (ICBMs) (450 missiles and silos total), and up to 120 fielded nuclear bombers.[1] As it stands, this plan will cost close to $400 billion and account for roughly 5 percent of the total costs of the next 10 years of defense spending, alternating roughly between 5 percent and 7 percent each year.[2] The Congressional Budget Office (CBO) expects modernizing the whole nuclear arsenal to cost roughly $1.2 trillion over the 2017–2046 time period.[3]

The majority of the nuclear modernization plan was crafted and put into action by the Obama administration.[4] In turn, the Trump administration inherited that plan and added its own requirements and alterations.[5] When the plan was first formed, then–Secretary of Defense Ashton Carter said that for many of these decisions, "It's not a choice between replacing these platforms or keeping them; it's really a choice between replacing them or losing them."[6] He likely intended to garner support for the expansive plan by underlining that capabilities without plans for revitalization will be lost.

However, his statement also drew attention to the fact that now is the perfect time to reassess all aspects of the U.S. nuclear arsenal. The systems funded and produced now will stay in the arsenal for the next 30 to 50 years, given the increased lifespan of technology. Nuclear modernization will require a large percentage of annual budgets for the foreseeable future; it is eminently possible that the current plans for overhauling nuclear assets could end up competing for funding with conventional priorities.[7]

Bad timing has created a large group of investment priorities that will all require considerable resources—if the next few administrations stay the course. Over the next 30 years, the Pentagon plans to drastically increase the number and complexity of ships in the navy, overhaul the makeup of the air force by retiring a significant number of older planes in favor of new acquisition projects, and increase the size of the active duty army—which will create sizable follow-on personnel costs.

Now is the time to look critically at all these best-laid plans, because they could derail each other without adequate attention. This chapter will examine the current modernization proposals, question their tenets, and provide a range of policy options that would allow for cost savings and reinvestment in the future force.

The Plan, as It Stands

To recapitalize the nuclear triad, the Department of Defense (DoD) and the Department of Energy (DOE) crafted nearly 20 major LEPs and entirely new systems that will be implemented over the next few decades.[8] These programs are in varying stages of development and require several phases of funding over the next 30 to 50 years (see Figure 1.1).

To upgrade the ground leg of the triad, the nuclear modernization plan calls for developing a new ICBM, known as the Ground Based

Figure 1.1

Cost of nuclear forces under the 2017 plan, 2017 to 2045

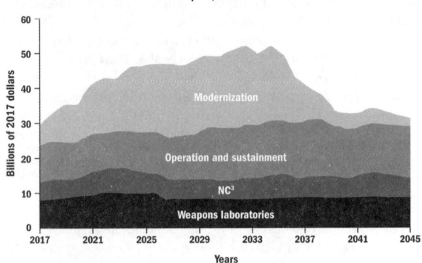

Source: Bennett, *Approaches for Managing the Costs of U.S. Nuclear Forces*, Figure 1.

Note: NC³ = nuclear command, control, communications, and early-warning systems.

Strategic Deterrent (GBSD), and renovating all current ICBM silos and associated infrastructure. The sea-based leg of the triad will consist of 12 *Columbia*-class SSBNs armed with refurbished Trident D5 submarine-launched ballistic missiles (SLBMs) equipped with updated W76 and W88 warheads. For the air leg, the modernization plan includes two new capabilities, the B-21 Raider bomber aircraft and the Long-Range Standoff (LRSO) cruise missile. There is also a planned LEP for the B61 gravity bomb known as B61-12.[9]

All three legs of the nuclear triad—SLBMs deployed on SSBNs, bombers, and land-based ICBMs—are valued for different reasons: SSBNs for their survivability, bombers for their flexibility and recall ability, and ICBMs for their numbers and price tag per unit.[10] But these three legs do not contribute the same value to deterrence.

Submarines can access most of the world's surface area and therefore provide the range of bombers with minimal losses to flexibility

3

of deployment.[11] As of today and for the foreseeable future, other nations cannot reliably track U.S. ballistic missile submarines—let alone do so with the sort of reliability required to attempt a preemptive strike against all of them at the same time.

Bombers maintain flexibility of the nuclear arsenal as they are yet another mobile leg of the triad.[12] However, this leg is easier for other nations to find, track, and target—so these weapons are less survivable than assets placed on SSBNs. Although they are easier to track, they can also be recalled once launched, and they boast high accuracy. Bombers can also serve as dual-use platforms for both nuclear and conventional weapons.

ICBMs provide the fewest advantages and contribute the least to overall deterrence. In theory, ICBMs add to strategic deterrence by increasing the overall number of targets that an adversary would need to eliminate in a first strike against the United States.[13] But if SSBNs cannot be reliably tracked and bombers provide more flexibility as mobile targets, ICBMs become less important as we move away from Cold War dynamics into a multipolar world with most nuclear powers fielding substantially smaller and less diversified arsenals.

Changes to the Ground Leg of the Triad

To build a future force equipped to handle the strategic situations of the next 30 to 50 years, the triad must evolve. The United States no longer faces a monolithic nuclear threat as it did during the Cold War, and it operates in a much more restrained fiscal environment today. The most obvious and necessary alteration to the current mix of capabilities is drastically altering the triad's ground leg. This leg makes up a large portion of the overall warhead count and includes up to 400 deployed and 50 nondeployed ICBMs in immobile silos located in Montana, North Dakota, and Wyoming.[14]

In 2017 the CBO released a report analyzing options for managing the cost of modernizing the nuclear weapons arsenal. It found that completely eliminating the ICBM leg of the triad would reduce the ability of the United States to engage in a large-scale nuclear exchange.[15] The 2018 *Nuclear Posture Review* notes, "In the absence of our ICBM force, a large proportion of our strategic nuclear triad, including SSBNs in port and non-alert bombers, could be subject to an attempted nuclear first strike involving a relatively small number of nuclear weapons."[16]

The goal of nuclear deterrence is to never enter into a nuclear exchange. If ICBMs are only useful in increasing the number of targets to be destroyed in a large-scale exchange, then nuclear deterrence, diplomacy, and all the safeguards against this type of conflict will have failed. Although a large-scale nuclear first strike involving that many warheads may have been a legitimate fear and thus required strategic planning in the past, this type of nuclear conflict scenario seems less likely today and in the foreseeable future.

While great power politics has returned to the fore of U.S. military strategy, a bolt-from-the-blue nuclear attack by Russia is improbable; China, in turn, does not possess a large enough arsenal to attack America's ICBM fields and have enough forces left over to hold U.S. cities at risk.[17] Moreover, the most likely scenarios that could draw the United States into conflict with Russia and China are limited conventional fights, not the large-scale invasion scenarios that worried U.S. nuclear planners during the Cold War. North Korea and Iran, both rogue states with varying degrees of nuclear capabilities, are often cited as more immediate nuclear threats. But Iran has yet to develop nuclear weapons, and North Korea maintains a small and unsophisticated arsenal that cannot threaten the U.S. triad with a disarming attack.[18]

It stands to reason that in the next 30 to 50 years, large-scale first-strike nuclear exchanges are unlikely to occur. A secure and robust SSBN fleet, rather than the ICBM force, is arguably the most important component of the triad for preserving America's second-strike capability. Former Secretary of Defense William Perry has argued this very point, saying that ICBMs are no longer essential to nuclear deterrence because "any sane nation would be deterred by the incredible striking power of our submarine force."[19]

Under current conditions, the strategic need to modernize and expand the ICBM force is much lower than when the leg was established during the Cold War. This change in strategic circumstances creates a valuable opportunity to modify our force structure moving forward and to move toward a leaner, more agile arsenal while accruing the financial benefits of limiting ICBM recapitalization.

OPTION ONE, MINIMAL ALTERATION: Cutting the ground leg by 50 percent.

This option would cut the ICBM force in half—fielding 200 missiles instead of the 400 currently deployed. That recommendation would lead to $19 billion in cost savings over the next 30 years, according to the CBO.[20] This estimate does not include an offset for retiring ICBM warheads early, because decommissioning costs are already built into the 30-year plan as older systems are phased out. There would be no immediate need to decommission all the ICBMs at once; they could be gradually phased out until the force has been reduced by 50 percent.

The United States currently operates 450 missile silos distributed over three military bases.[21] As with all follow-on options, reducing the ICBM leg by 50 percent would likely result in additional savings from base closures. Since only 250 silos would be required, 200 silos could be shut down or repurposed.[22] However, the estimated savings from this proposed change do not account for reduced overhead because it is unclear how or when the remaining forces would be redistributed.

Option one would leave most of the current plan intact but cut down on the number of new missiles procured over the next few decades. Strategically, this option would have very little impact. The triad would be slightly leaner but still fully functional and prepared for a large-scale nuclear exchange.

OPTION TWO, MODERATE ALTERATION: Cutting the ground leg by 75 percent.

This option would reduce the ICBM force by roughly 75 percent; the ICBM force would drop from 400 deployed missiles to 100. The CBO estimates that this change would create an overall savings of $27 billion over the course of the whole modernization plan.[23] The U.S. military prefers to sustain 50 more silos than fielded warheads—so this option would also theoretically create extra savings from closing roughly 300 silos (leaving 150 instead of the current 450 silos).[24]

Option two would leave the triad intact but significantly cut down on the number of new warheads procured as well as the investment needed to refurbish and maintain the entire associated infrastructure. As with option one, decommissioning costs are already built into the current plans, and building down to 25 percent of the current force could occur gradually through attrition.

OPTION THREE, LARGE ALTERATION: Cutting the ground leg entirely.

ICBMs may be relatively cheap to maintain, but severing this leg would save even more. The CBO estimates that fielding a dyad without the ICBM leg would create huge cost savings over the next 30 years. In terms of modernization program costs alone, the United States would save $88 billion in 2017 dollars.[25]

When taking into account total savings—reduced modernization as well as reduced operational and support costs—the figure rises to $120 billion or roughly 10 percent of total projected costs over the next 30 years.[26] Completely cutting the ICBM force would also allow for additional cost savings from shuttering all former silos and repurposing the bases for commercial use.[27]

Moreover, this estimate is based on fielding current forces until the end of their service lives and then decommissioning them. If this change was implemented immediately, more savings could accrue to the tune of an additional $29 billion dollars—bringing the total to roughly $149 billion over the next 30 years.[28] These savings primarily come from canceling the current LEPs for the existing force and then reaping the benefits of lowered costs for operating, sustaining, and supporting that force.

Changes to the Air Leg of the Triad

Over the next 30 years, the federal government plans to spend roughly $266 billion on the air leg of the triad. This includes all expenses associated with modernizing systems, as well as the cost of operating and supporting them. The current force structure includes 46 B-52s and 20 B-2s—the B-1 fleet was recently relieved of its nuclear mission under the U.S.-Russia New Strategic Arms Reduction Treaty (New START) agreement.[29] These systems have been part of the force structure for decades and function well together. Overall, they have benefited from several LEPs over their service lives and are expected to be in the force for several decades to come.[30]

The Department of the Air Force intends to add a new bomber to the fleet within the next 10 years. The B-21 Raider, formerly known as the Long Range Strike Bomber, is a stealth bomber that will eventually be fielded as a dual-use platform for both nuclear and conventional missions.[31] Very little is known about the budgetary implications for this system because it is a special-access (i.e., highly classified) program and thus not included in unclassified documents.[32] The bomber is currently in the research, development, test, and evaluation (RDT&E) phase, and Congress has allocated less than $5 billion annually to the plane's development over the last few years. However, with procurement starting in the 2020s, overall program costs will rise rapidly as the air force buys roughly 100 aircraft into the late 2030s.[33]

OPTION ONE, MINIMAL ALTERATION: Changes to planned missile development and forgoing the nuclear certification for the F-35A.

The military plans to add a nuclear mission to the repertoire of the F-35A combat aircraft despite repeated problems—especially in the fighter's system development and performance.[34] But adding another mission set to an arguably overburdened platform would be unwise. Because the current modernization plan retains the rest of the bomber fleet (B-52s and B-2s) through the 2040s and 2050s, respectively, and the B-21 Raider will be in full operational capacity by then, there is little need to add another type of delivery system to the air leg of the triad. The submarine leg of the triad covers any operational advantage in terms of stealth, and heavier existing bombers already achieve the flexibility and signaling that the air leg provides.

The bomber leg is scheduled to include several upgrades to the nuclear bombs themselves. The B61 gravity bomb is slated for another LEP that will consolidate almost all the existing models of the B61 into a singular design, known as the B61-12, that is compatible with both the B-2 and B-21 bombers as well as the F-35A. The LRSO cruise missile is also currently in the research and testing phase of development. It boasts a longer-range, flexible yield and is designed to survive advanced integrated air defense systems.[35] In contrast, the B61-12 can be fielded on tactical aircraft and has only mild ground-penetrating capability. For these reasons, it makes sense to continue investing in the development of the LRSO and not the B61-12.

Eliminating the nuclear mission for the F-35A provides another good reason for canceling the B61-12 LEP in its entirety. The B-2 and B-21 bombers will have other compatible missiles to use, while the B61-12 modifications primarily support the F-35's nuclear mission. The savings accrued from all of the above changes would be roughly $27 billion over 30 years.[36] The CBO estimate for this change includes $6 billion in savings from canceling the current B61-12 LEP. The remaining $21 billion in savings can be garnered from forgoing the F-35A's nuclear mission and the costs of maintaining the fighters with that certification. That $21 billion also includes the operational and support costs of the B61-12 and forgoing another LEP currently scheduled for the 2030s.[37] Option one would maintain the current B61 bombs to deploy on B-2s and B-21s until the LRSO is fielded—an investment of $5 billion to ensure that B-2s retain their nuclear mission in the interim.[38]

OPTION TWO, MODERATE ALTERATION: Delaying the program by 10 years and buying the full 100 planned B-21 bombers.

Another change that could produce significant savings in the near term would be delaying the modernization program by 10 years. This recommendation is designed to optimize the use of our existing force structure before retiring the current capabilities. The B-52s and B-2s that make up the current bomber wings of the nuclear triad are scheduled to remain part of the force until roughly 2040 for the B-52s and sometime in the 2050s for the B-2s, so delaying production of the B-21 Raider until the 2030s would not result in a substantial reduction in capabilities.[39] The B-21 could seamlessly transition into the force as the B-52s retire and still share the skies with the B-2s for 20 or more years. (See Figure 1.2.)

Figure 1.2

Approximate timelines for modernization of nuclear forces, 2015 to 2045

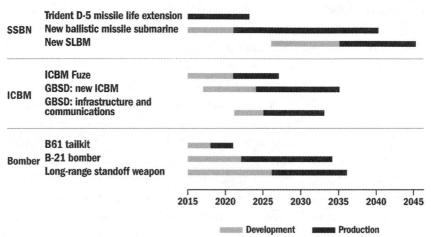

Delivery system life extensions or replacements

SSBN	Trident D-5 missile life extension	
	New ballistic missile submarine	
	New SLBM	
ICBM	ICBM Fuze	
	GBSD: new ICBM	
	GBSD: infrastructure and communications	
Bomber	B61 tailkit	
	B-21 bomber	
	Long-range standoff weapon	

2015   2020   2025   2030   2035   2040   2045

Development   Production

Source: Bennett, *Approaches for Managing the Costs of U.S. Nuclear Forces*, Figure 2.

Note: GBSD = Ground Based Strategic Deterrent; ICBM = intercontinental ballistic missile; SLBM = submarine-launched ballistic missile; SSBN = nuclear ballistic missile submarine.

This recommendation aims to align the procurement window of many of the B-21s with the procurement time of other systems. As Figure 1.2 shows, the B-21 development and production coincide with upgrades to the other legs of the triad. Delaying production by 10 years would get more time out of the service life of the current bomber fleet and save money in the short term for other competing funding priorities. Overall, this change would save roughly $37 billion over the next 30 years but extend the B-21s' production past the 30-year window, accruing costs into the 2050s.[40]

OPTION THREE, LARGE ALTERATION: Delaying the program by 10 years and capping development at 80 B-21 bombers.

Early plans for the B-21 involved procurement of 80 to 100 planes.[41] Because of other changes to the nuclear force structure and competing budgetary priorities, capping the procurement at 80 planes makes financial and strategic sense. This option would still procure the system within reasonable parameters of the current modernization plan but keep the number at the lower end of the spectrum. A nuclear bomber force comprising 20 B-2s and 80 B-21s would still be larger than the current fleet of 66 planes.

Option three would produce savings up front by virtue of buying 20 fewer planes, and it would lower operational and support costs over those planes' service lives. Publicly available data suggest that stopping production at 80 planes rather than 100 would generate savings of roughly $11 billion to $13 billion in procurement alone based on a hypothetical eight-per-year production schedule and a $564 million per-unit cost.[42] All in all, delaying the timeline by 10 years and capping the program at 80 planes would produce roughly $50 billion in total savings over the 30-year period. This option would not reduce any RDT&E or military construction funding for this program. However, if the strategic environment were to change, this option could be easily adapted to buying the full 100 planes in the out years, simply by keeping the production lines open longer.

Changes to the Sea Leg of the Triad

As the current modernization plan stands, the government will spend the largest piece of the budgetary pie on modernizing the sea leg of the triad. Over the next 30 years, the U.S. Navy will spend $313 billion on the SSBN force—$79 billion on maintaining existing systems and $234 billion on adding new platforms and systems.[43]

The current force of *Ohio*-class submarines includes 14 SSBNs, although at any given time 12 are deployed and two are in maintenance facilities.[44] The military plans to start retiring the *Ohio*-class as the first of the new-generation *Columbia*-class become operational. The oldest of the *Ohio*-class will begin exhausting its nuclear reactor fuel just as the production and procurement of the *Columbia*-class ramps up in the 2020s.[45] This timing should lead to a relatively seamless transition between the two generations of technology.

The military plans to procure a total of 12 *Columbia*-class submarines— replacing two fewer submarines than the current force structure.[46]

11

This program is still in the RDT&E phase, with funding levels scheduled to ramp up soon.[47] As it stands, the government plans to buy one unit every few years until the mid-2020s, when the pace increases to one submarine per year. This program will be costly—but to sustain America's credible nuclear deterrent, it is a necessary investment in force structure and capabilities.

The government already plans to spend close to $17 billion in fiscal years 2018–2022 on RDT&E and early stages of procurement. After that five-year period, the system will require more than $100 billion in procurement funds to build all 12 submarines, then an additional $133 billion in operations and support costs over their service lives (estimated at 40-plus years).[48]

The submarine force constitutes the most crucial leg of the triad overall. Thus, it is a priority not just strategically but also in terms of funding. Therefore, all options for altering this part of the modernization plan are offered in the context of alterations to the other legs. Minimal or moderate alterations to the ground and air forces would free up considerable resources that could be saved or partially reinvested in the submarine force. However, given current budgetary realities, investing more in the sea leg of the triad will not be feasible without downsizing elsewhere. This section draws attention to the need to set priorities in U.S. nuclear force structure and the gains that can be achieved by realigning those priorities.

OPTION ONE, MINIMAL ALTERATION: Stay the current course with SSBN procurement while reducing by 50 percent the ICBM leg and forgoing the nuclear certification of the F-35.

The current plan for SSBN procurement will ensure that the sea leg of the triad remains strong for the foreseeable future.[49] To offset some of the enormous costs associated with overhauling the sea leg of the triad, the two other legs should be altered.

The Government Accountability Office, among others, has questioned the financial feasibility of the current modernization plan, citing significant differences between policy and budget numbers.[50] Reducing the ICBM force by 50 percent and forgoing the nuclear mission for the

F-35A and associated missile systems would make a significant difference in how funding can be allocated. Changes to the ground leg would produce $19 billion in savings, while changes to the air leg would accrue another $27 billion over the next 30 years. Together, these alterations would give the nuclear force structure almost $50 billion in budget breathing room.

Under current fiscal realities, competing priorities will lead to friction and necessitate hard decisions. Option one aims to sustain funding for the current plan for the sea leg's modernization by downsizing the other two legs without fully decommissioning either.

OPTION TWO, MODERATE ALTERATION: Invest in two more SSBNs while cutting 75 percent of the ICBM force and delaying the B-21.

Implementing some of the other options to reform the nuclear triad would free up a considerable amount of funding for both cost savings and reinvestment in other areas. While this suite of options does not entail reallocating *all* the savings produced by reducing other capabilities, it would use *some* of those funds to increase the *Columbia*-class procurement by two submarines.

Procuring another two SSBNs in the 30-year time period would increase costs by $16 billion but increase the size of the force from 12 to 14, matching current capabilities.[51] The overall goal with this alteration is to increase the flexibility of the fleet and allow for increased maintenance and depot time if necessary.

Combining moderate alterations to the ground and air legs would produce enough savings to acquire additional assets for the sea leg while keeping the triad intact and functional, making this option more fiscally feasible. This would mean sustaining 100 fielded ICBMs in the ground leg and maintaining the existing fleet of B-52s and B-2s through the end of their service lives until the B-21 makes its operational debut.

Moderate alterations to the air leg would come from combining the $27 billion from forgoing the F-35's nuclear mission with the $37 billion in savings from delaying the B-21 procurement by 10 years. The CBO estimates that reducing the ICBM force by 75 percent over the next 30 years would result in another $27 billion in savings.

In total, moderate alterations to the other legs of the triad would free up $91 billion over the next 30 years. Some of those savings could feasibly be reinvested in the nuclear architecture to buy the most survivable leg of the triad more flexibility. Procuring two more *Columbia*-class SSBNs over the next 30 years would cost an additional $16 billion, leaving $75 billion in savings.

OPTION THREE, LARGE ALTERATION: Invest in four more Columbia-class SSBNs while cutting 100 percent of the ICBM force and delaying/capping the B-21.

In line with the moderate option, this large alteration is the culmination of three sets of major changes to the current modernization plan. Leaving aside political feasibility in the current budgetary environment, this option details what could be achieved through a significant reorganization of assets and requirements.

This option would take the U.S. force structure from a triad to a dyad by eliminating the ICBMs that constitute the ground leg and their entire associated infrastructure. This option is a substantial departure from current plans but would produce savings of $149 billion over 30 years. These savings would be combined with those from eliminating the planned nuclear mission for the F-35 ($27 billion), delaying the B-21 procurement by 10 years ($37 billion), and capping the B-21 procurement at the lower end of the acceptable range—at 80 planes rather than 100 ($13 billion). Together, these changes would total $226 billion in cost savings.

Option three would use some of that $226 billion saved to add four additional submarines to the planned SSBN fleet, bringing the total to 16. This investment would cost $30 billion, making the net savings $196 billion.[52] This alteration would be a significant change in force structure that would favor the sea leg while keeping the air leg intact and modernized, albeit on a delayed build schedule to accommodate the upfront costs of the *Columbia*-class program.

Conclusion

Ultimately, the most politically feasible of these options would result in minor alterations to the 30-year nuclear modernization plan. But any of these changes, however big or small, would set the United States on a better track to a sustainable and reliable nuclear force structure that would serve national security interests for the foreseeable future.

These options are all intended to align strategy with resources and fiscal reality. Sustaining America's nuclear deterrent capabilities and ensuring that U.S. forces can face any threat will always be a costly endeavor. Poor planning has led the nuclear and conventional bow waves to coincide in an era when annual defense budgets cannot grow much more without dangerously affecting the country's debt and deficits.

Policymakers cannot simply increase the defense budget to allow for all the added funding needed to accomplish every aim in the 30-year nuclear modernization plan. Those with the power to decide must also factor in the other conventional capabilities currently being requested: a 355-ship navy, a 386-squadron air force, a 540,000-strong active-duty army, and the creation of a space force. The time to prioritize is now, not when crucial assets meant to work together end up competing for funding.

2. It Can Get You into Trouble, but It Can't Get You Out

Missile Defense and the Future of Nuclear Stability

Eric Gomez

Missile defenses have come a long way since the Cold War. Then, the superpowers controlled inaccurate, nuclear-armed interceptors. Now, an ever-growing number of countries—including some that do not possess nuclear weapons—have more accurate, hit-to-kill systems in their inventories. The United States possesses the most advanced missile defense system by a wide margin, fielding a combination of regional systems that protect forward-deployed military units in addition to capabilities that purport to protect the entire U.S. homeland from limited nuclear attack.[1] Nonetheless, the threatening missile capabilities of potential adversaries combined with strong political support in Washington for better defenses are driving both qualitative and quantitative improvements to U.S. systems.[2] The Missile Defense Agency (MDA) received a record appropriation of $11.5 billion in fiscal year 2018.[3] The Trump administration's *2019 Missile Defense Review* (MDR) outlines a wholesale expansion of U.S. missile defense capabilities to counter the offensive missiles of both rogue states and great powers. Examples of new capabilities mentioned in the MDR include a space-based sensor layer for earlier missile detection, unmanned aircraft that can disrupt missiles with onboard lasers, and a missile defense mission for the F-35 aircraft.[4] While the primary targets of U.S. missile defense systems are rogue states such as Iran and North Korea, steady improvements in America's defenses are also a point of concern for China and Russia.[5]

Washington's plan to expand missile defenses combined with its focus on great-power competitors have important implications for nuclear stability. During the Cold War, there was a general understanding that limitations on nuclear weapons had to go hand in hand with limitations to missile defense. If neither side possessed an effective defense, then neither could gain a decisive advantage in a large-scale nuclear exchange by attacking the other's nuclear forces first and then absorbing the retaliatory blow with missile defenses.[6] The United States and the Soviet Union were highly sensitive to one another's missile defense developments, even if an effective defense was technically and economically infeasible at the time.[7]

The desire to protect the U.S. homeland against attack by rogue states such as Iran and North Korea has overtaken Cold War–era concerns about the destabilizing effects of missile defense since 2002, when the United States withdrew from the Anti-Ballistic Missile Treaty. However, attempts to reassure China and Russia that they are not the intended targets of steady U.S. missile defense expansion have not mollified either nation. Both China and Russia cite U.S. missile defense as a major contributor to their own nuclear force structure and strategy decisions.[8] The United States will probably not be able to construct a missile defense system capable of reliably protecting against even limited nuclear attack, but that won't stop other great powers from regarding U.S. missile defenses as a threat. Furthermore, the steps that other great powers take in response will further erode nuclear stability by increasing the risk of inadvertent escalation.

This chapter examines how proposed changes to U.S. missile defense systems will likely affect nuclear stability with other great powers. I argue that adversaries' threat perceptions are a more important driver of their behavior than the technical shortcomings of U.S. missile defenses. Thus, I recommend retaining U.S. capabilities for defending against shorter-range threats while forgoing enhanced homeland missile defense to slow the current slide toward nuclear instability.

The Present and Future of U.S. Missile Defense

America's missile defense architecture is designed to protect the United States as well as its allies and forward-deployed troops from limited attack. Current U.S. missile defense systems can be divided into two broad categories: regional defense systems and homeland defense systems.

Regional missile defense capabilities protect relatively small swaths of territory or high-value targets such as bases and command-and-control facilities from shorter-range ballistic missiles.[9] Usually, regional missile defense systems engage incoming missiles in the terminal stage of flight as the missile or its warhead falls to earth near its target, although some regional systems can engage targets in the midcourse phase of flight (e.g., SM-3 IA, IB, and IIA on Aegis warships). Another defining technical characteristic of regional missile defense is the systems' mobility. Ground-based interceptors such as the Patriot and the Terminal High Altitude Area Defense (THAAD) systems can be transported by military cargo aircraft.[10] The Aegis ballistic missile defense system uses several types of interceptors carried in warship vertical launch cells. As of fiscal year 2018, 38 U.S. Navy ships were missile-defense capable.[11] The United States frequently takes advantage of this mobility to quickly deploy systems to reassure or protect allies during crises.[12] Regional missile defense systems also tend to be more reliable than their homeland defense counterparts. According to the MDA, as of December 2018, the THAAD system had a perfect record in intercept flight tests, and the Aegis system had 40 successful intercepts in 49 attempts (81.6 percent success rate); the homeland defense Ground-based Midcourse Defense (GMD) system only had 10 intercepts in 18 attempts (55.5 percent success rate).[13] Moreover, the regionally focused Patriot system is the only component of the U.S. missile defense architecture that has intercepted ballistic missiles in combat, albeit with mixed success and against relatively unsophisticated adversaries.[14] Testing records are an imperfect indicator of future performance since systems are upgraded to account for shortcomings revealed by tests. However, the discrepancy between the GMD and regional defense systems indicates that intercepting shorter-range ballistic missiles is relatively easier than intercepting longer-range missiles that can strike the United States.

As the name implies, homeland missile defense capabilities aim to protect U.S. territory from intercontinental-range ballistic missiles (ICBMs). Whereas the United States has several types of regional missile defense interceptors (e.g., Patriot, THAAD, and Aegis), the 44 interceptors of the GMD system are the only option for defending the United States from ICBM attack.[15] This small stock of interceptors depends on widely distributed sensors, including early-warning satellites and various land- and sea-based radars, to have a reasonable chance of successfully engaging attacking warheads.[16] The GMD's poor reliability in missile defense tests means that in a combat scenario, multiple interceptors would have to be launched per attacking missile to maximize the chance of a successful intercept.[17]

The small size and unreliability of the GMD should reassure other great powers that their nuclear arsenals can effectively hold the U.S. homeland at risk, thereby bolstering nuclear stability. However, Washington is not satisfied with the current state of its missile defense systems. Many of the proposed improvements to U.S. missile defenses currently under consideration are meant to overcome the limitations and shortcomings that give China and Russia confidence in the effectiveness of their own nuclear arsenals.

Proposed improvements to U.S. missile defense capabilities prioritize homeland defense by expanding the number of interceptors and developing new technologies to provide more options for defeating intercontinental-range missiles. Congress has already approved funding to expand the number of GMD interceptors from 44 to 64 by 2023 and to start construction on new radar sites to improve the GMD's ability to differentiate between incoming warheads and missile debris or countermeasures.[18] The MDA is also developing the Multi-Object Kill Vehicle, a miniaturized version of the single, large kill vehicles carried by GMD interceptors.[19] If this capability performs as advertised, one GMD interceptor could engage multiple targets, marking a significant increase in the overall capacity of the system.

More exotic technologies for improving homeland missile defense currently under consideration include lasers carried by unmanned aircraft that destroy ICBMs before they leave the atmosphere, as well as cyber and electronic warfare capabilities that disrupt missiles before they are launched.[20] Of course, even strong political and budgetary support for new missile defense technology does not guarantee that current research and development efforts will come to fruition. The history of U.S. missile defense is replete with grandiose projects that ended up being scaled down or canceled and cutting-edge technology that failed to live up to expectations. However, near-peer adversaries like Russia and China will try to stay ahead of U.S. developments to keep their nuclear deterrent force effective. Those reactions to missile defense will have a greater effect on nuclear stability than missile defense itself.

Missile Defense, Adversary Perceptions, and Nuclear Instability

Missile defense is neither inherently stabilizing nor destabilizing. Rather, the effect of missile defense on nuclear stability depends on how defensive capabilities factor into a country's broader strategy. If a country possesses a large arsenal of offensive weapons in addition to a well-developed missile defense architecture, it will encourage perceptions that the country wants to achieve decisive nuclear superiority and make itself immune from retaliation. Nuclear stability is further affected by the counter strategies countries adopt in response to missile defenses.

American missile defense capabilities are destabilizing because they are just one part of a broader suite of systems that the United States can use to destroy adversary nuclear forces in a possible first strike. By themselves, U.S. missile defenses are unable to offer meaningful protection. However, alongside the United States' sizable arsenal of highly accurate offensive conventional and nuclear strike capabilities, America's limited missile defenses look much more menacing.[21] These offensive and defensive capabilities are part of an approach to nuclear strategy known as damage limitation. If the United States can limit—or potentially eliminate—the damage it would suffer in a nuclear war by destroying a substantial share of an adversary's nuclear forces and then use missile defense to intercept those that survive a first strike, then it will enjoy a dominant position vis-à-vis other nuclear powers.[22]

The fear of one-sided nuclear vulnerability is an important driver of Chinese and Russian reactions to U.S. missile defense. Although U.S.

21

defensive systems are currently ineffective and limited, Washington's push to expand their size and sophistication plays into the perception that it seeks nuclear superiority.[23] The perception that the United States wants to hold other nuclear-armed states at risk while insulating itself from damage is a far more important driver of Chinese and Russian threat perceptions than the shortcomings of current U.S. missile defense technology.[24] The United States argues that its missile defenses are incapable of protecting against the Chinese or Russian nuclear arsenals. But those arguments fall on deaf ears because they do not adequately account for either adversary's concern that future defenses might have that capability—in which case China or Russia would be in grave danger of a U.S. disarming first strike.[25]

Nuclear stability is further damaged by the counter strategies that China and Russia are implementing to keep their nuclear arsenals viable in the face of improved U.S. missile defenses and offensive strike systems. Neither country seems interested in significantly increasing the size of its nuclear forces to raise the probability that enough warheads could both survive a disarming attack and overcome defensive systems.[26] Such a buildup could spark an arms race with the United States, but it could also improve nuclear stability by making adversaries less worried about U.S. missile defenses and other damage-limitation capabilities.[27]

Additionally, a larger nuclear arsenal reduces incentives for escalation within a conflict. For example, in a hypothetical war between China and the United States, Chinese ballistic missile bases would be a high-priority target given their ability to attack U.S. air and naval bases in the region.[28] However, some of China's bases house missiles that can carry either a nuclear or conventional payload. An American attack intended to destroy a conventional missile unit would run the risk of destroying a nuclear unit instead, which could in turn be interpreted as the start of a broader U.S. effort to eliminate China's nuclear forces.[29] The unintentional destruction of one nuclear missile unit would be less threatening, from Beijing's perspective, if the country built up its nuclear forces; a larger arsenal could absorb the loss and remain viable as a retaliatory force. Thus, having a larger arsenal would reduce pressure on Chinese leaders to respond to such an attack with nuclear weapons out of fear that any hesitation might lead to the loss of their entire nuclear deterrent.[30]

Neither China nor Russia is really trying to build its way out of nuclear vulnerability. Instead they are taking two other steps to counter the expansion of both U.S. missile defense and, more broadly, damage-limitation capabilities. First, they are introducing new technology to improve the ability of their nuclear weapons to penetrate U.S. missile defenses. One such technology is the hypersonic glide vehicle (HGV), which approaches its target on a less predictable trajectory than a ballistic missile warhead and is therefore more difficult to successfully intercept.[31] Both China and Russia are pursuing HGVs, and worries of falling behind in a new arms race have spurred U.S. efforts to develop both its own HGV systems and research new missile defenses to protect against adversary capabilities.[32] Russian leader Vladimir Putin recently unveiled other examples of new nuclear capabilities designed to defeat U.S. missile defense, including a nuclear-powered cruise missile and a nuclear-armed underwater unmanned vehicle.[33]

Many of these counter-missile defense technologies are not fully developed, and some will likely fail to deliver their expected benefits. However, investments in these capabilities signal Russian and Chinese concerns about the strategic implications of U.S. missile defenses.[34] Both potential rivals are clearly worried about the ability of their nuclear forces to defeat U.S. defenses—despite current technical shortcomings of U.S. systems—and they are devoting considerable effort and resources to staying a step ahead.

The second step China and Russia are taking to counter U.S. missile defense expansion is to adopt military strategies aimed at reducing the U.S. military's situational awareness in order to quickly win limited, conventional conflicts in areas where the stakes are higher for them than for the United States. These strategies are not explicitly focused on making the United States more vulnerable to nuclear attack. Rather, they are meant to bring about a quick victory over local U.S. forces and present Washington with a fait accompli: either accept a small defeat or absorb considerably more pain to reverse it. Degrading U.S. situational awareness by destroying or disrupting systems such as land-based missile defense radars or early-warning satellites is a high priority for potential adversaries because the U.S. military depends heavily on such capabilities to fight modern wars.[35]

These military strategies have dangerous implications for nuclear stability. Many of the capabilities essential for situational awareness—and likely near the top of Russian and Chinese target lists—are not exclusively used for conventional operations. In the words of James Acton of the Carnegie Endowment for International Peace: "[These capabilities] are typically dual use; that is, they enable both nuclear and nonnuclear operations. Second, they are increasingly vulnerable to nonnuclear attack—much more vulnerable, in fact, than most nuclear-weapon delivery systems."[36] For example, Chinese leaders have an incentive to destroy U.S. missile defense radar sites in East Asia because doing so would make China's conventional offensive missile operations in a regional conflict more effective.[37] However, some of these radar sites also provide data to homeland missile defense interceptors that protect the United States from nuclear attack.[38] A similar problem exists in outer space. The same satellites that provide Washington with early warning of a nuclear attack are used to cue missile defenses against conventional ballistic missiles.[39] Reducing U.S. situational awareness would naturally fit into adversary conventional war plans, but such attacks increase the risk of inadvertent nuclear escalation by appearing to target U.S. nuclear command and control—even if that wasn't the object. Just as Chinese and Russian leaders could reasonably interpret attacks on their forces as a prelude to a wider assault on their entire strategic deterrent, so too might U.S. officials react to attacks on critical sensors as the first move in a broader nuclear attack.

America's current and planned missile defense architecture are bad for nuclear stability. The pursuit of bigger and better missile defenses stokes fears that the United States is uninterested in deterrence and instead seeks nuclear superiority. China and Russia are developing technologies and implementing military strategies in response to U.S. missile defense that make conflicts more prone to inadvertent nuclear escalation. Maintaining the current trajectory of missile defense expansion will only exacerbate these destabilizing effects, making future crises more dangerous at a time when U.S. relations with both potential adversaries seem likely to deteriorate for the foreseeable future.

Balancing Missile Defense and Nuclear Stability

Setting restraints on U.S. missile defense capabilities, especially systems that defend the continental United States, could help slow or even reverse the erosion of nuclear stability with other great powers. Moving away from homeland defense would allow the U.S. military to focus on developing and fielding systems optimized to counter shorter-range missiles. Such a change in missile defense policy would improve nuclear stability by reducing adversary "use-or-lose" pressure in crises while also making it harder for adversaries to initiate limited, regional conflicts.

Restraining homeland missile defense is a sensible policy shift for both technical and strategic reasons. America's only homeland defense system—the GMD—has the worst testing record of all currently deployed missile defense systems.[40] Current technical shortcomings can presumably be solved, but the effort to develop and deploy the various improvements will take a great deal of time and money—and there is no guarantee the new technology will live up to expectations.[41] Expanding the GMD while pursuing new homeland defense capabilities will only deepen Russian and Chinese concerns that the United States is building up missile defense to make their own nuclear arsenals ineffective, which in turn will encourage them to make counter moves that increase the risk of nuclear war.[42] Setting restraints on homeland missile defense should be a low-hanging fruit for U.S. policymakers.

A restrained posture could entail a range of options, from capping the capacity of existing systems to eliminating them entirely. While either caps or divestment would be strategically sound, caps are more politically expedient given current legislative and executive branch support for missile defense. Introducing a hard ceiling on the number of deployed GMD interceptors would be a good first step for limiting homeland missile defense. According to current plans, by 2023, 64 GMD interceptors will be deployed across two sites, with most (60) in Fort

Greely, Alaska.[43] Capping the number at 64 would provide a degree of protection against limited nuclear threats, such as North Korea. At the same time, a cap would increase the credibility of U.S. assurances that missile defense cannot reliably defend against more sophisticated arsenals and therefore does not undermine the credibility of China's or Russia's nuclear deterrent.

However, since China and Russia have not been swayed by U.S. promises to date, merely setting a cap would not be sufficient. Washington would also have to reclaim its position as a leader in arms control to make the GMD cap more compelling. Using the GMD cap as a carrot to get other great powers to agree to similar limitations on their own missile defense systems, for example, or to launch negotiations on strategic transparency, would underscore Washington's commitment to nuclear stability even if its broader relationships with China and Russia deteriorate. The diplomatic and political opportunities created by an interceptor cap would be a much more valuable tool for reinforcing nuclear stability than the cap itself.

A more ambitious form of American restraint would be a complete divestment from homeland missile defense. Divestment would entail dismantling all GMD interceptors, abandoning research and development on boost-phase defenses that engage enemy missiles as they begin flight, and forswearing interceptors in outer space. In this scenario, the various sensors that support homeland missile defense would be solely focused on other missions, such as providing early warning of nuclear attack or tracking objects in orbit.[44] Complete divestment from homeland missile defense would send a strong signal to other near-peer competitors that the United States does not wish to negate their nuclear arsenals.

Divestment from homeland missile defense would reinforce nuclear stability in two ways. First, if rival great powers have faith in the effectiveness of their second-strike nuclear forces, they will not face strong pressures to use their nuclear forces quickly for fear of being disarmed. Reducing this so-called use-or-lose incentive makes crises less prone to nuclear escalation. Second, taking the homeland missile defense mission away from U.S. early-warning satellites would help clarify the escalation risks of attacking these systems; the link between attacks on U.S. early-warning capabilities and the risk of a U.S. nuclear response would be much more direct. This clarity would increase the costs of Chinese or Russian offensive action in outer space, which is a more effective way to deter attacks than the current U.S. approach that entangles nuclear and nonnuclear systems in that domain.[45]

Moving away from homeland defense does not mean that the United States would have to give up on missile defense entirely. In fact, without a homeland missile defense capability, regional missile defenses are far less dangerous for nuclear stability and could even bolster it. Regional missile defense already enjoys one benefit over its homeland defense counterpart: it works.[46] Systems that defend relatively small areas from shorter-range threats have much more successful testing records than the GMD, and some regional systems such as Patriot and Iron Dome (an Israeli system made with considerable U.S. support) have enjoyed some success in combat.[47] Shifting funding toward proven technology and away from the ineffective GMD and other dubious homeland missile defense systems would be a far more efficient use of defense dollars.

Strategically speaking, a more robust regional missile defense architecture can buttress nuclear stability by making it harder for great-power adversaries to win quick, conventional wars. American military bases and communication facilities would be high-priority targets of Russian and Chinese missile capabilities in the opening stages of a conflict. Current regional missile defense interceptors, coupled with emerging missile defense technologies like high-powered microwaves and solid-state lasers, could create densely layered protection for these fixed, ground-based targets.[48] Those capabilities would raise the costs of attack and reduce the likelihood of rival great powers initiating fait accompli military action against the United States. Meanwhile, the absence of U.S. homeland missile defense would reduce adversary fears of a rapid U.S. counter escalation that could destroy the adversary's nuclear forces.

An expansion of U.S. regional missile defense is conducive to nuclear stability only if the United States also moves away from homeland

27

missile defense. Stronger regional missile defense raises the costs of initiating limited conflicts. If a great power decides to initiate a conflict anyway, regional missile defenses would help slow down the pace of the conflict and reduce the risk of inadvertent nuclear escalation. The lack of a U.S. homeland missile defense shield would also engender a more restrained U.S. approach to a hypothetical conflict by raising the risks of military strikes against enemy nuclear forces. In other words, stronger regional missile defense coupled with weaker homeland missile defense should help prevent the most likely form of great-power conflict in the 21st century and help keep any conflict that does break out from escalating to a nuclear exchange.

Conclusion

Missile defense gets the United States into trouble, but it can't get us out. The steady expansion of the U.S. missile defense architecture has fostered destabilizing counter strategies by America's great-power rivals without providing systems capable of protecting the United States from the consequences. Forging ahead with missile defense expansion will only cost more money while further eroding nuclear stability at a time when U.S. relations with both Russia and China are deteriorating.

This approach is unsustainable and dangerous. To arrest these trends, Washington should divest itself of ineffective and destabilizing homeland missile defense systems and devote its effort and resources to improving regional missile defense systems that protect smaller areas. Such a shift will reassure rivals that America does not seek nuclear dominance over them while also making it more difficult for them to go on the offensive in the hope of winning quick conflicts. This approach is a more effective use of taxpayer money and has better implications for nuclear stability than continuing to expand all aspects of U.S. missile defense.

3. The Risks a War in Space Poses for Nuclear Stability on Earth

Todd Harrison

The Soviets successfully launched the first orbiting satellite, Sputnik I, in 1957 during a time of high tensions between the United States and the Soviet Union. Both nations were rapidly expanding their nuclear arsenals and fielding land- and sea-based intercontinental ballistic missiles (ICBMs)—weapons that could be launched with little warning, were largely unstoppable, and could reach their targets within minutes. It was a new era of strategic competition with weapons that were not yet well understood and space capabilities that were still in their infancy.

From the beginning, nuclear forces and space forces were closely interrelated—a relationship that evolved throughout the Cold War and fundamentally changed in the post–Cold War era. This chapter examines the role of space systems in overall U.S. military strategy, the development and proliferation of systems to counter the space assets of other nations, also known as "counterspace" capabilities, and how deterrence in space (or the lack thereof) can affect nuclear deterrence on Earth. It concludes with several policy options designed to reduce the risks of conflict in space and the effects such conflict could have on nuclear stability.

Deterrence in the First Space Age

The United States and the Soviet Union dominated the first space age, with the two superpowers accounting for 93 percent of all satellites launched from 1957 to 1990.[1] Space became a contested domain in 1959 when the United States conducted the first known anti-satellite (ASAT) test. A Bold Orion missile launched from a B-47 aircraft flew within a few miles of a target satellite. While the test missile was not equipped with a nuclear warhead, it proved that a nuclear-armed missile could get close enough to destroy a satellite.[2] Three years later, the United States detonated a 1.4 megaton nuclear weapon in space as part of the Starfish Prime experiment.[3] The Soviets were working in parallel on their own "counterspace" systems, mainly co-orbital ASAT systems that could gradually maneuver close to a target satellite and detonate a conventional warhead.[4]

Because the space race began during a period of heightened nuclear competition, it was somewhat inevitable that the competition in space would be linked to the nuclear arms race already under way on Earth. Roughly 70 percent of the satellites launched during the first space age were for military purposes, and most were used to support nuclear forces.[5] The United States and the Soviet Union used intelligence collection satellites to keep track of each other's missile production facilities, missile launch sites, and air defense systems, among other things. Each nation deployed its own constellation of missile warning satellites for early detection of missile launches, making it possible to launch a counterattack before missiles arrived at their targets, which added credibility to the idea of mutually assured destruction. Both sides also used communication satellites to maintain assured command and control of nuclear forces even if terrestrial cables and transmission sites were destroyed.

The two superpowers quickly became dependent on space to support their respective nuclear forces, but these space systems were vulnerable to attack by ASAT capabilities—weapons that both sides had developed. This mutual vulnerability became an important stabilizing factor that led to several treaties and agreements. For example, the Starfish Prime test in 1962 led directly to the Partial Test Ban Treaty in 1963.[6] In 1971, the Accidents Measures Agreement between the United States and the Soviet Union required immediate notification of interference with missile warning and related communications systems, and the Hotline Modernization Agreement required both sides to protect the Direct Communication Link between the U.S. president and the Soviet premier.[7] And as part of the Anti-Ballistic Missile Treaty of 1972, both countries agreed not to interfere with each other's means of verification, which included reconnaissance satellites.[8]

This détente in space had some unintended consequences for the designs of satellites and the types of orbits used by the U.S. military. The physicist and overhead reconnaissance expert Amrom H. Katz summed it up well in a now-declassified paper written for the National Reconnaissance Office in 1972:

> We are embarked on a course of development that produces and deploys bigger and bigger, more and more complex, longer and longer life systems. These birds have been protected by assumption—the belief that nobody would interfere with their operation. Even in the absence of evidence that the assumption rests on questionable premises, it should have been clear that the line of development we were pursuing—a predictable manifestation of U.S. style—might by itself greatly influence or change the other guy's behavior. Said simply, we are tempting him with juicier targets than we used to.[9]

As Katz adroitly observed, the space architectures the U.S. military built during the first space age—the types and numbers of satellites, the way they operated, and the orbits they occupied—rested on the assumption that if nuclear deterrence held on Earth, deterrence would hold in space. At the time, this was a reasonable assumption since space was primarily used to support nuclear forces. Other than the Soviets, few nations had the ability to attack U.S. space systems. And regardless, there was little to be gained by attacking U.S. satellites in anything other than a nuclear conflict. Thus, the United States continued to build small quantities of large, complex, and expensive satellites that were designed to last for many years and with limited protections. In Katz's words, the U.S. military kept building bigger, juicier targets.

Deterrence in the Second Space Age

The end of the Cold War and the demise of the Soviet Union marked a turning point for U.S. nuclear forces and space forces. With the signing of the first Strategic Arms Reduction Treaty (START) in July 1991, both sides committed to reduce their nuclear forces by approximately 30 percent overall, with deeper reductions in some areas.[10] Rather than waiting for START to take effect, the United States accelerated the process by unilaterally removing all 450 Minuteman II missiles from alert status and terminating the mobile Peacekeeper ICBM development program.[11] Subsequent negotiations and treaties continued to make reductions in nuclear forces and ultimately reduced the overall role of nuclear weapons in U.S. national security strategy.

As these nuclear reductions occurred, the ways in which the U.S. military used space evolved into what has been termed the "second space age."[12] The 1991 Gulf War demonstrated for the first time the decisive role that space-based capabilities could play in a conventional conflict. Bombs and missiles guided by the Global Positioning System (GPS) demonstrated an unprecedented level of precision; missile warning satellites supported the Scud-hunting campaign to find and eliminate Iraqi ballistic missiles; and satellite communications gave field commanders a new level of connectivity and situational awareness. The U.S. military's appetite for space-based capabilities quickly became insatiable. For example, the demand for satellite communications bandwidth was estimated to be 100 megabits per second (Mbps) in the 1991 Gulf War, 250 Mbps in Joint Task Force Noble Anvil in Kosovo in 1999, 750 Mbps in the early months of Operation Enduring Freedom in Afghanistan in 2002, and 2,400 Mbps in the opening phases of Operation Iraqi Freedom in 2003.[13] As the military became more dependent on space for conventional combat, many of the space systems that were originally intended to support nuclear forces began to take on more nonnuclear missions. For example, missile warning satellites and protected communications satellites were routinely used to support conventional forces by providing highly secure, jam-resistant communications for maneuver forces and early warning for theater ballistic missile launches.

Other militaries soon took notice of the many advantages space provided for the United States in conventional operations across the full spectrum of conflict. They recognized that the U.S. military's success in integrating space capabilities into its conventional military operations created a vulnerability because these systems were largely designed with a Cold War mindset. They were "protected by assumption," as Katz had noted decades earlier—an assumption that the possibility of starting a nuclear war would deter an adversary from attacking U.S. space systems.[14] The U.S. military's dependence on space and its lack of robust protections from a range of counterspace weapons created an opportunity for adversaries to exploit.

Threats to Space Systems

What changed in the second space age is not that space became contested—space has been contested since the first ASAT test in 1959. What is different now is that the United States is not as confident in its ability to deter attacks against its space systems. U.S. space systems are used for far more than supporting nuclear forces, and the idea that an attack on these systems could precipitate a nuclear war no longer holds the same credibility as it did during the Cold War. Moreover, the threats to space systems are growing and proliferating, in part because ongoing U.S. vulnerabilities in space create a strong incentive for adversaries to acquire counterspace capabilities. Perhaps the seminal event that brought this issue to the forefront of strategic thinking was the 2007 ASAT test in which China destroyed one of its own satellites and produced a cloud of debris, much of which lingers in orbit to this day.[15]

The threats to space systems, however, are not limited to direct-ascent ASAT attacks like the Chinese test. Counterspace weapons also include co-orbital systems that can maneuver into a target satellite or otherwise interfere with its operations; jammers and spoofers that can disrupt the radio frequency communications going to or from a satellite; cyber threats that can infiltrate ground systems and potentially affect the command and control of a satellite; and directed energy weapons, such as lasers that can blind the sensors on a satellite and high-powered microwaves that can damage sensitive electronics. Importantly, many of these counterspace weapons are no longer the exclusive domain of technologically sophisticated nation-states like Russia and China. Iran and North Korea, and even some nonstate actors, are increasingly acquiring counterspace capabilities.[16]

One of the challenges this creates is that some of the most highly proliferated counterspace capabilities are reversible forms of attack for which timely attribution can be difficult. Jammers, for example, can be difficult to detect and geolocate in an already noisy radio frequency environment. The U.S. military has noted that it inadvertently jams itself dozens of times each month.[17] Moreover, jamming is fully reversible—once the jammer is disengaged, communications can be reestablished. The problem for military planners is how to deter or respond to such an attack if the effects are temporary and the attacker knows it cannot easily and quickly be identified and stopped.

The rising threats to U.S. space systems present a challenge for nuclear deterrence because many military space systems are used for both nuclear and nonnuclear missions. In a conventional conflict, an adversary may seek to disrupt or destroy U.S. space systems that are being used to support conventional military operations against it, even if these systems are also used to support nuclear forces. If missile warning satellites, for example, are being used to detect theater ballistic missiles in a conventional conflict, an adversary may attempt to blind the infrared sensors on the satellites. During the Cold War, such an act would have been viewed as a prelude to a full-scale nuclear attack and potentially could have led to a nuclear response. But the threat of nuclear retaliation in response to an attack on a U.S. space system that is being actively used in conventional military operations is not as credible. The dual-use nature of many space systems can lead to mistakes and miscalculations in a crisis that could escalate a conventional conflict into a nuclear crisis.

One of the complications in the space domain is the lack of widely accepted "norms of behavior." International agreements are limited, and the main international treaty that governs space—the Outer Space Treaty—is more than 50 years old. This treaty explicitly prohibits the establishment of military bases and the testing of weapons on the moon or other celestial bodies, and it prohibits the placement of nuclear weapons in orbit. But it does not prohibit the use of orbital space for military purposes, the placement of conventional weapons in orbit, or the intentional damage or destruction of satellites.[18] And unlike the other warfighting domains, in space there is little experience or history to draw upon—especially warfighting experience—to understand what types of actions should be considered threatening or hostile.

As a result, the thresholds for escalation in space are unclear in many areas. Ambiguous thresholds can invite aggression as adversaries probe at the seams and push the limits of acceptable behavior. Over time, an adversary could condition other nations to accept aggressive behavior in space as normal. For example, Iran, North Korea, and others routinely jam satellite communications and GPS signals without provoking a military response. This raises the question: What type of jamming *should* trigger a military response and under what circumstances? And what is a proportionate response to such an attack?

Options for Policymakers

The United States has so much at stake in space—both militarily and commercially—that its primary objective should be to deter conflict from extending into space, and, if deterrence fails, to bring conflict in space back to Earth as quickly as possible. Policymakers should look at three ways to help improve the United States' deterrence posture in space.

First, the United States should rethink the architectures used for national security space systems and stop building big, juicy targets. Next-generation space systems should be designed with enhanced protections across the full spectrum of counterspace weapons. Space systems can be better protected in many ways. For example, communications satellites can use waveforms that better resist jamming, and satellites can incorporate greater shielding from electromagnetic pulse and high-powered microwave weapons.[19] Another method of protection is to distribute capabilities across more assets. For example, instead of using a small number of exquisite satellites in geostationary orbit, the U.S. military could deploy large constellations of smaller, less sophisticated satellites in a variety of orbits that, in aggregate, can perform the same mission. Space architectures can also be enhanced by using hosted payloads (i.e., taking a simplified version of the payload—sensors, communications, etc.—from a military satellite and hosting it on other commercial or international partner satellites). In a distributed architecture, the value to an adversary of taking out any one satellite is much less, making each satellite a less attractive target.

Second, the United States should reconsider the policy of using certain space systems for both nuclear and conventional missions. At the end of the Cold War, aggregating conventional and nuclear missions on the same satellites made sense because of the overlaps in capabilities and the budget savings that aggregation allowed. Dual-use systems may continue to make sense for some missions, but they can complicate the strategic calculus for both the United States and potential adversaries. An adversary might target an attack against a system for its conventional role, but the United States could interpret the attack as being targeted against the nuclear mission of that same system and respond with a higher level of escalation. The United States should explore options to disaggregate nuclear and conventional missions from space systems where it is practical and strategically feasible.

A third area for policymakers to reexamine is the thresholds for escalation of conflict in space. Because many national security space systems support both conventional and nuclear missions, the escalation ladder for a conflict in space is inherently intertwined with the escalation ladder for nuclear conflict. Escalation thresholds for attacks against space systems need to be understood internally to inform contingency planning and the development of retaliatory options. Where appropriate, thresholds need to be effectively communicated to adversaries and allies alike to avoid miscalculation and miscommunication in a crisis.

Conclusion

Throughout the Cold War, the close connection between nuclear forces and space forces was a stabilizing factor. Space-based capabilities made the verification of nuclear arms control agreements possible and reduced mistrust on both sides, while the cloak of nuclear deterrence helped prevent conflict from extending to the space domain. But in the post–Cold War era, the close coupling of nuclear and space capabilities has become a potentially destabilizing factor. U.S. space systems are essential to conventional military operations across the full spectrum of conflict, and the threat of nuclear retaliation is no longer a credible deterrent. Establishing a more stable deterrence posture in space is vital to prevent a conflict that extends into the space domain from escalating into the nuclear domain.

4. U.S. and Russian Nuclear Strategies
Lowering Thresholds, Intentionally and Otherwise
Olga Oliker

Russian and American nuclear strategies are inherently intertwined. As the two countries with by far the world's largest nuclear arsenals, the United States and Russia cannot help but factor one another into their planning. A decade or two ago, this connection may have seemed like a historical artifact. Today, however, with relations deteriorating rapidly, officials in both countries have become increasingly unlikely to claim that the other is irrelevant to their nuclear strategy or force posture. The United States' 2018 *Nuclear Posture Review* (NPR) cites Russian strategy as a justification for the United States to build new nuclear capabilities, including a low-yield submarine-launched ballistic missile warhead and a new sea-launched cruise missile.[1] Meanwhile, for two years in a row (2018 and 2019), Vladimir Putin's annual address to the Russian parliament has highlighted new strategic weapon systems touted for their capacity to respond to the American threat.[2]

If Russia and the United States are both building weapons and planning for their possible use with the other in mind, are their actions informed by reality or misperception? Do the two countries understand one another's strategies sufficiently to respond adequately, and do their views of what is "adequate" align? Most importantly, do their policy choices make us safer?

In this chapter I argue that Russians and Americans view each other's statements, force postures, and strategies through their own assumptions and plans, leading to distortion. This phenomenon is exacerbated by both countries' desire to embrace ambiguity and by disconnects between force posture and policy. The policies that result threaten to weaken, rather than strengthen, deterrence. The solution lies in less reliance on nuclear coercion and ambiguity and more on direct communication. Avoidance of lower-yield and dual-capable systems by both countries would also contribute to stability.

Perceptions and Interpretations

The Russian understanding of the American approach to conflict is predicated on a concept of "air-space war," which, despite the name, is more rooted in air than in space capabilities.[3] Usefully and succinctly described by prominent Russian analysts Alexey Arbatov, Vladimir Dvorkin, and Petr Topychkanov, "air-space war" assumes that the United States will bring the full scope of its air dominance to bear on a conflict, in part to avoid ground contact with the adversary. This assumption is rooted in the patterns that Ministry of Defense planners and other Russian analysts have identified in U.S. warfighting over the past quarter century, including in the former Yugoslavia, Iraq, Libya, and Syria.[4] From the political perspective, Russian analysts see Americans using tools of national power, including military tools, to compel other governments—or remove them from power. Moreover, America seems to view any disagreement with its policies, anywhere in the world, as a threat.[5] Put this concept of "air-space war" together with the many unpleasant things U.S. leaders have said about both Russia's government and its policies. Then the Russian view—that, at some point when the two countries disagree, the United States could well decide to dispatch shock and awe from above to force Moscow to capitulate—becomes plausible.

In the event of a U.S. attack, Russian planners believe that Moscow will be at a conventional disadvantage, despite recent improvements in Russia's air defenses and other capabilities. This relative weakness will make Russia vulnerable to coercion by the United States.[6]

Russian strategists also expect that the United States will target Moscow's nuclear capabilities early in such a conflict to prevent nuclear retaliation. Along with the air power barrage, their thinking goes, America will likely launch conventional precision attacks against Russian nuclear forces and command and control capabilities. These attacks might be combined with nuclear strikes if American conventional weapons are not sufficient to accomplish the task. If such attacks take place with little warning, Russia's strategic nuclear forces could be thinned out to the point that a retaliatory strike could be absorbed by American missile defenses.[7] The Russian understanding of this approach is plausible in part because the United States has made clear that its nuclear war plans call for first strikes against an adversary's nuclear capabilities, also known as a counterforce strategy.[8] In the United States, this strategy is often couched in moral arguments (i.e., it is more moral to target weapons than people).[9] However, a counterforce strategy is inherently a first-strike strategy, with the intent to limit damage to oneself in the probable, large-scale nuclear exchange that comes later.

None of this is new to Russian thinking.[10] Very recently, however, perhaps in light of America's 2018 NPR and its call for the development of new low-yield nuclear weapons, an interesting shift has occurred. While past Russian writing emphasized the threat that American conventional capabilities pose to Russia and its nuclear forces, today some Russian analysts are arguing that the NPR indicates that the United States is looking to develop and deploy more usable (or "ecologically acceptable") nuclear weapons.[11]

The open source literature in the United States on Russian strategic nuclear doctrine is thin. However, in recent years, American policymakers and some prominent experts have stated that Russia intends to use tactical nuclear weapons to seek rapid, lower-cost victory in a heretofore conventional conflict.[12] Those who believe that this is likely envision a scenario in which, for example, Russia attacks a Baltic country and uses smaller-yield nuclear weapons to demonstrate resolve when U.S. forces come to assist the victim.[13]

One reason to think this is Russia's strategy is that, indeed, Russian writings and some military doctrine, particularly naval doctrine, discuss "de-escalatory" strikes—nuclear and otherwise. Western analysts who hold this view of Russian strategy (such as Elbridge Colby, Matthew Kroenig, and Katarzyna Zysk, and, apparently, the authors of the NPR) also argue that Russian military exercises practice so-called de-escalatory nuclear strikes and note Russia's recent predilection for developing systems capable of carrying both nuclear and conventional payloads.[14]

Their arguments are further bolstered by the tendency of Russian government officials to highlight their country's nuclear capability when Moscow seeks to change other countries' behavior—and when talking about the United States.[15]

The core of Western concerns about Russia's perceived nuclear strategy, however, may lie less in Russian plans and capabilities and more in the fear that this strategy could work: a credible threat to use tactical nuclear weapons in the early stages of a conflict could weaken America's will to defend North Atlantic Treaty Organization (NATO) allies, especially the Baltic states. In short, the United States does not want to be deterred by the threat of nuclear escalation from a conflict with Russia that it might otherwise embark on.[16]

Responses

For Russians who believe that the United States has conventional superiority and is willing to launch a substantial strike against Russian nuclear weapons, an emphasis on Moscow's nuclear arsenal as the ultimate guarantor of security and sovereignty makes sense. Without nuclear weapons, after all, what would keep Russia from suffering the same fate as Yugoslavia?[17] While Russians debate whether the United States could truly deliver a disarming first strike, few Russian analysts believe that existing American missile defenses are sufficient to protect against a Russian second strike.[18] What drives Russian fears is the belief that if the United States cannot do this now, it will be able to do so soon enough.[19] To ward off this possibility, Russia has increased the proportion of its strategic nuclear warheads on more survivable systems—namely, ballistic missile submarines and mobile intercontinental ballistic missiles (ICBMs)—rather than vulnerable silo-based ICBMs (although it is also building new silo-based ICBMs, like the Sarmat). In their rhetoric, Russian officials frequently play up the ability of these and other new weapons to overcome missile defenses. Putin made precisely this point in his March 2018 speech to the Russian parliament, now famous for its emphasis on the development of a range of new weapon systems.[20] Additionally, Russia has increased its emphasis on early-warning and air defense capabilities, as well as, to a lesser extent, its own missile defenses. Finally, Moscow continues to press the United States to return to the negotiating table to reintroduce limits on missile defenses.[21]

Meanwhile, in the United States, the view of Russian strategy as esca-latory has spurred calls for developing new low-yield nuclear capabili-ties of America's own. Indeed, the 2018 NPR uses Russia's perceived strategy as a rationale for the United States doing just that: "expanding flexible U.S. nuclear options now, to include low-yield options, is important for the preservation of credible deterrence against regional aggression" because it "[signals] to potential adversaries that their limited nuclear escalation offers no exploitable advantage."[22]

American proponents of new lower-yield capabilities argue that their credibility is enhanced as numbers and variety grow.[23] But while Russia has a much larger arsenal of tactical or low-yield nuclear weapons than the United States, it is unclear why more low-yield nuclear weapons are needed to demonstrate U.S. resolve. After all, if the United States needs to demonstrate its will to respond in kind to a Russian small-scale use of tactical nuclear weapons, a handful of weapons (already in the arsenal) should be sufficient.

Realities

Russian and American views of each other's strategies are almost certainly somewhat distorted. While there is evidence to support some aspects of the Russian perspective on U.S. strategy described above, other components reflect unlikely, worst-case scenario assumptions. Available information indicates that, indeed, the United States has plans for the possible first use of nuclear weapons in certain cases, while also retaining the capacity to respond to an adversary's first strike.[24] How-ever, America's strong conventional capabilities bolster arguments that, despite these plans, the United States is highly unlikely to use nuclear weapons first. Moreover, the United States has been unhappy with the policies of many countries but has not bombarded them all with air strikes. So, an unexpected attack on Russia for which Moscow has had little time to prepare seems highly unlikely. That said, coercion, or at least coercive intent, does appear to be a factor in American nuclear planning and thinking.[25] And, of course, the decision to use nuclear weapons is solely at the discretion of the president, so a great deal depends on the predilections and preferences of a single individual.

Russia's overall military doctrine sets a high bar for nuclear use: a nuclear response can be triggered only by nuclear or weapon of mass destruction use by another state or in a conventional conflict "when the very existence of the [Russian] state is in jeopardy."[26] Russian military documents and statements by military officials indicate that Russian plans call for the use of nuclear forces either when the country is under attack or after it has been attacked.[27] Vladimir Putin himself has indicated that nuclear use is possible only if Russia sees enemy missiles approaching its territory.[28]

If we accept the doctrine's (and Putin's) word that Russia would use nuclear weapons only when it perceived a genuine, existential threat to its homeland and sovereignty, we can still imagine a few scenarios for first use. One would involve Russian preemptive action if it believed the United States was on the verge of launching a debilitating first strike. Such an expectation could trigger a large-scale Russian preemptive launch.[29] Others might include situations in which Russia expected an invasion or attack against the Russian homeland, which could lead the Kremlin to contemplate smaller-scale use to remind the Americans of the risks. Some military exercises appear to have included the use of bomber-delivered nuclear weapons practicing a first, limited nuclear strike if defeat seems imminent and Russia fears invasion.[30]

That brings us to nonstrategic nuclear weapons. While the use of nuclear weapons of any form would, of course, have strategic effects, this chapter treats long-range, high-yield intercontinental systems as "strategic" and shorter-range, lower-yield systems as "nonstrategic." While there is scant evidence of Russian planning to use nonstrategic nuclear weapons early in a conflict for strategic gain or easy victory, in the past Moscow *has* thought about the possibility of limited nuclear use to de-escalate a conflict. Indeed, Russian nuclear strategy around the turn of the century seemed to be something akin to "escalate to de-escalate": nuclear weapons, and the threat of their use, were meant to compensate for conventional weakness.[31]

But times have changed. In modern Russian doctrine, the closest approximation to this approach is found in Russia's 2017 naval strategy, which states that the fleet must be able to inflict no less than critical damage on an adversary's fleet with the use of nonstrategic nuclear weapons and that "under conditions of escalation of a military conflict, the demonstration of readiness and will to use force by means of non-strategic nuclear weapons is an active deterrence factor."[32] This language is convoluted, to be sure. It notably speaks of demonstration, readiness, and will, rather than direct use. Yet it also directly references a role for nonstrategic nuclear weapons in de-escalation. Importantly, this clause was not present in the previous, 2012 naval doctrine, which discussed de-escalation—but in the context of conventional, rather than nuclear, weapons.[33]

Does this change indicate that Russia has a high bar for strategic nuclear use but intends to use tactical nuclear weapons to gain the advantage in conventional conflicts? Perhaps, but probably not. The convoluted language of the 2017 naval doctrine is also in line with the concept suggested above: if Russia expects a conflict to threaten its sovereignty and territorial integrity, then tactical nuclear use, just like strategic nuclear use, would not be inconsistent with doctrine. This approach is not "escalate to de-escalate," as it is generally presented in the West, in that it is not a tactical mechanism to achieve battlefield benefit. Rather, this approach is rooted in the belief that some amount of escalation control is possible, or at least worth a try when all else has failed, and that tactical nuclear weapons can contribute. In summary, Russia's overall military doctrine sets a high bar for nuclear use. The naval doctrine, but only the naval doctrine, appears to set a somewhat lower bar.

What about capabilities and exercises? Russian tactical nuclear weapons are mostly kept in central storage, away from their delivery vehicles. Thus, they cannot be used on a whim. That said, the recent emphasis on new systems, such as the Iskander ballistic missile and Kalibr naval cruise missile, which can be deployed with nuclear or conventional weapons, means that an outside observer (or target) cannot be certain what is being launched until the warhead hits its target. Those who believe Russia is prone to nuclear use will see exercises incorporating these systems as demonstrations of the escalate-to-de-escalate approach. Conversely, observers who doubt that is Russia's strategy will see them either as conventional exercises or as exercises that simulate nuclear use in cases of a threat to Russia's existence. Vague, bellicose statements by Russian leaders suggest that they think nuclear weapons grant coercive advantages.[34] The bottom line is that Russia is most likely to use nuclear weapons when it sees a threat to its sovereignty, and it is likely to see that threat if it thinks it is losing a conventional war with the United States. Under those circumstances, a response using either tactical or strategic nuclear weapons is possible.

Implications

In sum, there is a disconnect between Russian perceptions and the reality of U.S. nuclear strategy, and vice versa. U.S. policymakers and strategists are focused on the prospect of limited Russian nuclear strikes in a conventional conflict and how to ensure that escalation is managed at a low level. Their Russian counterparts fear that the United States will launch a disarming first strike. Thus, plausible scenarios for armed conflicts involving the United States and Russia could lead Russian leaders to fear that, at any moment, the United States might attempt to disable Russia's ability to retaliate. Russians are not inclined to believe that the United States will stop short of trying to eliminate their nuclear arsenal; thus, they are probably also not inclined to believe that U.S. actions will be limited, at least not for long.

Of course, Russians may simply want Americans to *think* that Moscow cannot be restrained. George Mason University's Gregory Koblentz summarized the Russian position on Twitter: "When you go low yield, we go high yield."[35] But it's risky to be too sanguine when the stakes are this high. Putin's own comments about conditions for a retaliatory strike have included the presumably rhetorical question, "Why do we need such a world, in which there is no Russia?"[36] That is, if Russia is at risk, the world might as well be too.

If one believes that nuclear weapons are helpful in preventing conflict, then believing that the worst could happen is what makes deterrence work. If one thinks that escalation can be controlled and contained at lower levels, then one is surely less fearful, more likely to go to war, and more likely to use nuclear weapons.

Thus, from a mutual deterrence perspective, both states' policies are counterproductive and dangerous. Whatever Russia's actual bar for nuclear use, its emphasis on dual-capable systems and fondness for coercive rhetoric feeds U.S. fears of a lowered nuclear threshold. It also increases the risk that a U.S. conventional strike will lead to nuclear escalation or be perceived as a prelude to nuclear use.[37] Russia's leaders may think that they're strengthening their deterrent vis-à-vis the United States, but they are actually weakening it. Meanwhile, the U.S. interest in adding nuclear rungs to escalation ladders feeds a Russian perception that their smaller-yield nuclear weapons make Americans nervous. This perception, in turn, increases a Russian belief in the coercive power of nuclear threats and strengthens voices within Russia that see value in additional nuclear escalatory steps. All of this together creates an unnerving cycle, making us all less secure.

Solutions

The world would be a safer place if both Russia and America agreed to eschew nuclear coercion, avoid ambiguity, and stay away from low-yield, dual-capable weapons. Agreements to verifiably keep nonstrategic warheads away from their delivery vehicles, as Pavel Podvig and Javier Serrat recently proposed in a paper for the United Nations Institute for Disarmament Research, would also be helpful.[38] Unfortunately, neither Moscow nor Washington appear to have much appetite for new arms control agreements at present. Moreover, Russians have a lot invested in the Kalibr and Iskander missile systems, and there is no easy way to ensure that those cannot be deployed in a nuclear configuration.

While the challenges are many, even simple recognition of the problem could help mitigate it. If honest conversations about strategies and plans are too much to ask, unilateral steps remain possible. On the U.S. side, little can be gained from building new low-yield nuclear systems, which would only feed Russia's destabilizing tendencies.

45

America, with its tremendous conventional advantages, has no need to rely on low-yield nuclear weapons. Instead, placing more emphasis on nonnuclear capabilities could well push Russia toward adding conventional rungs to its own escalation ladder, in line with Russia's long-term military modernization plans. That emphasis and response, combined with the continuing shadow of strategic nuclear war, would strengthen deterrence and make conflict—including nuclear conflict—less likely.

5. U.S. Nuclear Strategy toward China
Damage Limitation and Extended Deterrence
Austin Long

The 2018 *National Defense Strategy* and *Nuclear Posture Review* (NPR) both make clear that the U.S. government believes it faces an era of renewed long-term competition with great powers, including China.[1] This competition includes a nuclear component, with the United States seeking to use its nuclear arsenal as part of an overall effort to deter potential aggression against itself and its allies. Yet the question of how the U.S. nuclear arsenal can best contribute to deterrence is open for debate. Should the United States seek the capability to neutralize, to the greatest extent possible, the Chinese nuclear arsenal as part of this competition? Or should it accept some degree of vulnerability with China, in order to prevent or reduce the destabilizing impact of potential Chinese responses?

Broadly speaking, one school of thought argues the United States should eschew the pursuit of such capabilities and accept mutual vulnerability with China. Charles Glaser of George Washington University and Steve Fetter, a former Obama administration adviser now at the University of Maryland, argue that U.S. efforts to acquire the ability to neutralize China's nuclear arsenal are unlikely to succeed but *are* likely to worsen the U.S.-China relationship, particularly in crisis.[2] Australian National University professor Hugh White goes further, urging the United States not only to forgo such capabilities but to make explicitly clear it is mutually vulnerable with China.[3]

Another school of thought emphasizes that the ability to limit damage to the United States and its allies enhances deterrence, particularly extended deterrence to allies, and can help achieve U.S. objectives even if deterrence fails. The 2018 NPR underscores the need for damage limitation generally in U.S. nuclear strategy, noting "U.S. nuclear policy for decades has consistently included this objective of limiting damage if deterrence fails."[4] Other analysts have likewise highlighted this need vis-à-vis North Korea.[5]

This chapter extends the damage limitation argument to China, arguing that a competitive nuclear strategy with China has both risks and benefits. It proceeds in four parts. First, it briefly defines the elements of a more competitive nuclear strategy with China. Second, it highlights the risks of a competitive nuclear strategy, namely the risk that both sides might believe they face pressure to use nuclear weapons early in a crisis. A competitive nuclear strategy could also incentivize the Chinese to accelerate and expand the growth of their nuclear arsenal. Third, it describes the benefits such a strategy has for enhancing U.S. extended deterrence commitments in East Asia. Finally, it argues for a competitive nuclear strategy that strikes a balance between these risks and benefits.

Nuclear Competition and Damage Limitation

The core of a U.S. competitive nuclear strategy with China is damage limitation, a concept born during the Cold War. While nuclear weapons are tremendously destructive, they are not infinitely so. A combination of air and missile defense, civil defense, and offensive strikes on adversary forces could greatly reduce the amount of damage an adversary's nuclear arsenal could inflict on the United States. For small adversaries, such as North Korea, it might even be possible to neutralize their arsenal entirely. For larger adversaries, such as China, complete neutralization is unlikely but very substantial reduction could be possible.[6]

China's current nuclear force structure and strategy are focused on preventing significant damage limitation by ensuring their ability to carry out retaliatory nuclear strikes against an adversary that attacks first. Most of China's nuclear weapons are based on mobile land-based ballistic missiles and ballistic missile submarines at sea, making them difficult to find and target. This strategy of "assured retaliation" is intended to discourage attacks on China as no attacker could do so without facing potentially massive destruction in return.[7]

Yet even though China's nuclear strategy is one of retaliation, in a crisis or conventional war, China's nuclear arsenal would cast a long shadow over the United States and its allies. If China began to lose, it could decide to escalate intentionally to nuclear use. This possibility could erode the credibility of U.S. deterrence and its assurances to allies.[8] A damage-limitation strategy would bolster the credibility of U.S. deterrence and assurance commitments to allies by making China's retaliatory capability less certain.

To implement a damage-limitation strategy, the United States would have to field a variety of offensive and defensive capabilities that could locate and destroy China's nuclear assets before and after launch, respectively.[9] Targeting mobile systems, such as submarines and mobile ballistic missiles, would require substantial additional investments in intelligence collection systems (e.g., satellites and stealthy drones to collect information and analytic capabilities to rapidly interpret raw data). Successful damage limitation would also require continued investment in missile defense as well as both nuclear and conventional strike systems. Finally, this strategy would demand investments in cyber and electronic warfare capabilities to disrupt Chinese command and control systems.

Even if Chinese leaders did not want or intend to escalate to nuclear use, a U.S.-China conventional conflict could put pressure on them to do so, resulting in inadvertent escalation. In this scenario, U.S. conventional attacks might unintentionally hit Chinese nuclear forces or nuclear command and control systems. In turn, Chinese leaders might believe that if they did not use nuclear weapons quickly, not only would they lose the conventional war, but Beijing's ability to carry out future retaliatory nuclear strikes could be seriously degraded by U.S. conventional weapons. This creates a "use-or-lose" incentive for the Chinese leaders.[10] Although at present Beijing appears relatively sanguine about the survivability of its arsenal, U.S investment in damage-limitation capabilities could exacerbate the use-or-lose incentive.[11]

Competition and the Dangers of Instability

The chief risk of a competitive U.S. nuclear strategy toward China is the potential damage it could cause to strategic stability. This term has a contested meaning but generally incorporates two subsidiary forms of stability.[12] The first is the concept of "first-strike stability," defined as the lack of either incentives or pressures to use nuclear weapons first in a crisis.[13] In a crisis characterized by perfect first-strike stability, leaders are indifferent to whether their nuclear forces are employed first or second as the results will be the same—and presumably equally catastrophic. Policies promoting first-strike stability are explicitly about reducing the use-or-lose incentive. First-strike stability helps avoid the problem of inadvertent escalation, to some degree. The second form of strategic stability incorporates the idea of "arms-race stability." Arms-race stability prevails when neither side of an adversarial relationship believes it must greatly expand the quantity or quality of its nuclear arsenal to maintain first-strike stability.[14]

If the United States pursues significant damage-limitation capabilities, then a potential nuclear crisis with China might become less stable, as Chinese leaders could believe they need to use nuclear weapons early in crisis or risk losing their ability to use the weapons at all. Current sanguine assumptions among Chinese experts of the low risks of nuclear escalation could be reversed if the United States expands its suite of damage-limitation systems.[15] Beijing may also begin expanding its nuclear arsenal at a much greater rate than the modest rise of the past two decades.[16] In that case the United States would be forced to invest even more in damage-limitation capabilities in order to stay ahead of Chinese developments.

Why Run the Risk? The Challenge of Extended Deterrence

With such risks, one might wonder why the United States would ever pursue such a capability. The answer, as with the Soviet Union in the Cold War and North Korea today, is to prevent the threat of Chinese nuclear use from undermining U.S. extended deterrence commitments, which could drive a wedge between the United States and its allies.

As RAND Corporation analysts Glenn Kent and David Thaler summed up at the end of the Cold War, there are inevitable tensions between stability and extended deterrence:

> The most important conflict arises between the objectives of enhancing first-strike stability, on one hand, and extending deterrence and limiting damage, on the other; i.e., the more robust the Soviets believe first-strike stability to be . . . , the less they might hesitate to precipitate a deep crisis by engaging in serious aggression. . . . Balancing between first-strike stability and extended deterrence presents a problem in the planning of strategic forces.[17]

This argument is predicated on the view that nuclear deterrence depends on the possibility that nuclear weapons might be used. As nuclear deterrence theorists Thomas Schelling and Robert Jervis have argued, nuclear crises are competitions in risk taking.[18] Greater risk tolerance thus translates into competitive advantage before and during crises. Damage-limitation capabilities can produce greater risk tolerance and, by extension, competitive advantage by reducing the confidence of an adversary in its nuclear retaliatory capability.[19] For this reason, the United States maintained damage-limitation capabilities throughout the Cold War. As the 1978 *Nuclear Targeting Policy Review* describes, *"The U.S. targets the Soviet nuclear threat to achieve two objectives: the first is limiting damage both to the U.S. and our allies; the second is to prevent the emergence of a post-war nuclear balance that would facilitate coercion by the Soviet Union."*[20]

The common argument against pursuing damage-limitation capabilities targeting China is that it is simply not feasible. No damage limitation could be 100 percent effective since the Chinese could make prudent counterinvestments to prevent it. Therefore, the argument goes, no U.S. president would ever actually risk a strike for damage-limiting purposes; the Chinese would know this; and damage limitation would carry all the risks and costs associated with it without improving deterrence.[21] However, this argument assumes the Chinese would know with high confidence what a U.S. president would do in a crisis that would by definition be almost without precedent. It also assumes the Chinese would effectively be able to keep pace with

U.S. investments in damage limitation. These are major and perhaps unwarranted assumptions.

A similar argument (and counterargument) was made during the Cold War about damage limitation vis-à-vis the Soviet Union. As the 1978 *Nuclear Targeting Policy Review* made clear:

> With respect to the damage limiting objective, today there are two distinct views. . . . One view holds that since we cannot expect to limit to low levels the damage resulting from a large scale nuclear attack, . . . it is no longer a meaningful objective and should be abandoned or at least given a low priority. . . . The opposing view is that we must continue to do the best that we can to protect the U.S. from the consequences of a nuclear war if deterrence fails. Given the uncertainties of nuclear war . . . there might well be situations where the capability to reduce damage by perhaps tens of millions of American lives would be far from futile.[22]

Yet we now know that the Soviet Union's ability to compete in the nuclear realm was more constrained than analysts realized during the Cold War. Despite holding a vastly larger arsenal than China presently has, Soviet leaders were not confident in their nuclear retaliatory capability in the late Cold War.[23] According to one source, by the early 1980s Soviet military leaders "deeply felt that the Soviet Union was substantially inferior in strategic weapons—in all systems—and that the best they could hope for was to preserve the status quo, and not to fall behind any more. What they wanted to try to do was hold on to the position that had been achieved by the time of, let's say, 1977."[24] Some Soviet political leaders believed this might also translate into U.S. competitive advantage. In 1981, Yuri Andropov—the head of the Soviet security agency, the KGB, and soon to be Soviet leader—argued in a private meeting with his East German counterpart: "The U.S. is preparing for war *but* it is not willing to start a war. . . . They strive for military superiority in order to 'check' us and then declare 'checkmate' against us without starting a war."[25] Indeed, Soviet leaders were genuinely concerned about the possibility of a U.S. attack in the period around 1983—the so-called war scare period—despite the massive Soviet nuclear arsenal.[26]

The Soviet case demonstrates that damage-limitation capabilities don't need to be 100 percent effective to increase risk tolerance and produce superior competitive advantage. Instead, the adversary must believe that damage-limitation capabilities are plausibly effective and that, in a crisis of the highest possible stakes, the state possessing such capabilities is more willing to gamble because it has some probability of limiting retaliation.[27] The prospects for such damage limitation hinge on technical factors, primarily the contest between command and control systems and counter–command and control systems (e.g., cyber or electronic warfare) as well as the contest between hiding (e.g., mobility, concealment, and deception) and finding (remote sensing and surveillance systems). While a full analysis of the prospects for this competition with China are beyond the scope of this essay, other analyses suggest the United States could prevail—or at a minimum that the Chinese may believe the United States could prevail.[28]

Moreover, a competitive U.S. nuclear strategy vis-à-vis China characterized by damage limitation could provide greater benefits than an alternative, less competitive approach. Such an alternative approach would rely primarily on U.S. and allied conventional capabilities supported by the possibility of U.S. limited nuclear use. Conventional capabilities are, in themselves, unlikely to be sufficient to deter China from initiating a crisis when it believes its vital national interests are at stake. For example, a crisis over Taiwan would carry very high stakes for China given the Chinese Communist Party's strong nationalist claims to the island. In such a crisis, Chinese leaders might well believe they have the superior political resolve and geographic proximity to prevail.[29]

Likewise, Chinese leaders might believe that the United States would be unwilling to proceed very far, if at all, in a series of limited nuclear exchanges. As James Schlesinger, then at the RAND Corporation but subsequently secretary of defense, wrote in the months preceding the Cuban Missile Crisis, "In a war of nerves, with limited encounters, which side will prove the stronger—especially when we have reached the city-swapping stage?"[30] Thus, if the United States accepts nuclear vulnerability and does not field damage-limitation capabilities, superior resolve could allow China to prevail in a crisis. Even if the Chinese were mistaken in their belief about the superiority of their resolve, they might nonetheless be willing to escalate a crisis into a conflict on the basis of this misperception, leading to a failure of deterrence.

Balancing Risks and Benefits

A competitive nuclear strategy focused on damage limitation could change Chinese perceptions about the risk of nuclear escalation, thus bolstering deterrence. The goal of such a strategy would be to make U.S. damage limitation look plausible in a crisis while, ideally, avoiding making any crisis extremely unstable. Kent and Thaler term this posture one of "optimum instability":

> Indeed, one might argue that an optimal amount of first-strike instability is possible: that is, enough to deter the Soviets from generating a major crisis . . . but not enough to allow a major crisis to spiral out of control. Whether or not such an optimum actually exists, the concept provides the proper intellectual framework in which to think about the trade-off between first-strike stability and extended deterrence.[31]

While such optimum instability may be a balance difficult or even impossible to achieve in practice, it provides the right framework for making competitive choices to improve U.S. damage limitation and extended deterrence. At the same time, the United States should make clear to Chinese leaders that damage limitation is a measure of last resort in a crisis rather than a perpetual threat. Conveying that idea would require significant diplomatic engagement with China, which has often been challenging on issues of strategic stability.[32]

The pursuit of this optimum instability would also have the benefit of forcing Beijing to make hard choices about its defense investments. Unless the Chinese military budget (and the economy that underpins that budget) grows infinitely, every dollar spent on ensuring the survivability of China's nuclear arsenal will trade off, at least to some extent, with some other military investment. For example, Chinese investment in ensuring the survival of its nuclear intercontinental ballistic missile force is money that cannot be spent on anti-access/area denial capabilities that have caused concern among some analysts.[33] Thus, rather than fueling an arms race, a more competitive nuclear strategy would shape a competition that, according to the U.S. *National Defense Strategy*, is already underway.[34]

Conclusion

Implementing a more competitive U.S. nuclear strategy against China requires many of the investments already outlined in the 2018 NPR, such as acquiring "robust adaptive planning to defeat and defend against attacks, including missile defense and capabilities to locate, track, and target mobile systems of regional adversaries."[35] The specific systems needed for this strategy require more detailed analysis but could include stealthy drones, advanced anti-submarine warfare, unmanned sensors, new surveillance satellites, and tailored cyber operations.[36] Allies can provide assistance by acquiring supplementary capabilities as well as providing geographic access and proximity for U.S. systems.

A greater challenge of a competitive nuclear strategy is reassuring the Chinese that substantial U.S. damage-limitation capabilities are not synonymous with an existential U.S. threat to China. The theoretical concept of "optimum instability" means creating enough instability in the U.S.-China nuclear relationship to bolster extended deterrence without making crises prone to spiral rapidly out of control. Finding that balance in practice will be a challenge. Yet the pursuit of optimum instability can offer substantial benefits over the course of strategic competition.

6. The Future of Extended Deterrence
Are New U.S. Nuclear Weapons Necessary?
Eric Gomez

The U.S. nuclear arsenal is the hardest working of its kind. Besides deterring attacks on the homeland—a standard feature of every nuclear arsenal in the world—U.S. nuclear forces are also on call to defend the territory of American allies in Europe and East Asia. These extended deterrence commitments have been an important feature of U.S. nuclear strategy since the start of the Cold War. And while the threats facing U.S. allies have changed since Washington first extended its nuclear umbrella, there are no signs that extended deterrence is going away anytime soon.[1]

In fact, the importance of both nuclear weapons and extended deterrence seems set to increase as the United States prepares for a return to great-power competition. Multiple strategy documents released by the Trump administration refer to Russia and China as major threats to the United States and its allies and focus American defense efforts, including U.S. nuclear strategy, on responding to these actors. As stated in the *2018 National Defense Strategy*, for example, "The central challenge to U.S. prosperity and security is the *reemergence of long-term, strategic competition* by . . . revisionist powers."[2] This focus on great-power competition is likely to continue beyond the Trump administration given a general worsening of U.S. relations with the two competitors and broad support for a tougher U.S. approach within the national security bureaucracy and Congress.[3]

Washington's desire to maintain its extended deterrence commitments during this so-called return of great-power politics will be a major driver of U.S. nuclear force structure in the years to come. According to the 2018 *Nuclear Posture Review* (NPR), nuclear weapons are likely to become a much more important factor in U.S. military strategy vis-à-vis

Russia and China.⁴ Using nuclear capabilities to bolster extended deterrence is a well-worn course of action for U.S. policy. But absent a broader discussion about the political challenges of extended deterrence under modern and future conditions, more nuclear weapons will just make existing challenges more dangerous. In other words, reaching for nuclear solutions to the new extended deterrence questions facing the United States is misguided. This is not to say that nuclear weapons won't have *any* utility in a new era of great-power politics, but overstating their value carries dangers of its own.

Instead of expanding U.S. nuclear capabilities in a bid to keep extended deterrence viable, U.S. strategists should be thinking about deterrence more broadly. Nuclear weapons are not the only tool that states can use to defend themselves from attack. The ability of allied countries to use nonnuclear capabilities to raise the costs of aggression by potential adversaries has improved as conventional strike and missile defense technology have advanced. These developments enable a "deterrence-by-denial" strategy, which resists enemy action by denying a quick, easy military victory for the attacking country. Instead of threatening an aggressor with massive punishment against population or industrial centers, deterrence by denial emphasizes defensive capabilities that can defeat or bog down the adversary's military should it go on the offensive. Moreover, if deterrence fails and conflict does erupt, relying more on modern nonnuclear capabilities can reduce the risk of nuclear escalation.

The Challenges to Extended Deterrence

The extended deterrence commitments the United States made during the Cold War are now subject to very different structural conditions. The United States formed several bilateral alliances in East Asia when China was economically poor and militarily weak. Although Beijing did obtain nuclear weapons in 1964, its deterrent was small and vulnerable until it began modernizing its nuclear forces in the 1990s.⁵ During the Cold War, American policymakers regarded China as a threat and considered taking military action against it on a number of occasions, but Washington enjoyed large advantages over Beijing, especially in naval and air power.[6] China's rapid economic growth since 2000 has led to a corresponding increase in military spending by Beijing. While the United States still enjoys advantages in both the amount of military spending and the quality of key military technologies, Chinese capabilities are increasingly sophisticated and able to present the United States with real challenges in limited regional conflicts.[7] Importantly, a recent slowdown in China's economic growth rate has not negatively affected either military spending or the pace of President Xi Jinping's military reforms that aim to improve the performance of the Chinese military in modern, high-technology conflict.[8]

Structural conditions in Europe have also changed since the end of the Cold War. America enjoyed a favorable balance of power in Europe after the collapse of the Soviet Union and ensuing Russian economic and military weakness. The United States took advantage of the situation, expanding the North Atlantic Treaty Organization (NATO) eastward to include former Warsaw Pact countries despite implicit promises made to Russian leaders in the early 1990s not to add these states to the alliance.[9] Expanding U.S. extended deterrence commitments closer to Russia's borders was a relatively low-cost, low-risk decision at the time. However, Moscow has clawed back some of its power in recent years. While Russia is still weaker than the United States in broad terms, improvements to both Russian nuclear forces and conventional capabilities pose challenges to the commitments that the United States made when Russia was too weak to muster opposition to U.S. actions.[10]

Further complicating the task of extended deterrence is the relative decline of U.S. power writ large. The high operational tempo and demand for forces created by the wars in Iraq and Afghanistan, and other lesser theaters of the Global War on Terror, have overworked the U.S. military and damaged general readiness. The United States remains the world's largest economy, but its share of global output is decreasing. According to data published by the World Bank, America's share of global gross domestic product decreased from approximately 27 percent in 1997 to 24 percent in 2017, while China's share grew from 3 percent to 15 percent over the same period.[11] Relative U.S. decline was to be expected as the Chinese economy rapidly grew and Russia got its house back in order after the collapse of the Soviet Union. Of course, the United States is still a very powerful state overall. However, the end of America's "unipolar moment" means that maintaining far-flung security commitments will grow more difficult over time.[12]

Nuclear Solution or Illusion?

The Trump administration wants nuclear weapons to play a more important role in U.S. foreign policy than did the three previous administrations—including with respect to extended deterrence commitments. At its core, U.S. nuclear force structure planning for the new period of great-power competition is driven by two beliefs: that escalation can be controlled, and that achieving and maintaining escalation dominance is in the United States' best interest.[13] In other words, to deter great-power adversaries, the United States needs a flexible nuclear force structure that will allow Washington to respond to a wide variety of contingencies and ensure that "any use of nuclear weapons, however limited, is unacceptable."[14] Two defining characteristics of such an arsenal are a prominent role for low-yield or "tactical" nuclear weapons and a wide variety of delivery options (cruise missiles, gravity bombs, ballistic missiles, etc.) across the three legs of the triad. Supporters of a flexible and diverse nuclear force structure argue that the range of options it provides for controlling escalation make it the best kind of nuclear arsenal for the United States, especially given the various nuclear and conventional capabilities that potential adversaries possess.[15]

Washington also regards a flexible nuclear force structure as necessary for making extended deterrence commitments credible. Despite President Donald Trump's frequent rhetorical fusillades against cheap-riding allies, U.S. policy under his administration has deviated little from that of his predecessors. Indeed, in some notable examples, U.S. material support to allies has increased since Trump took office.[16] The prevailing view in Washington is that flexibility enhances credibility by offering U.S. leaders more options to respond to adversary threats against allies short of a large-scale nuclear war. According to this logic, moving away from the large and diverse nuclear arsenal would weaken

U.S. extended deterrence commitments by reducing the credibility of U.S. nuclear threats. Were the United States to have a smaller nuclear arsenal, writes Keith Payne, a former deputy assistant secretary of defense, "an opponent's doubts about its credibility would render [U.S. nuclear threats] of little deterrent value."[17]

Moreover, countries covered by the U.S. nuclear umbrella can be very sensitive to changes in the U.S. arsenal that reduce American flexibility—even if the actual use of nuclear weapons to defend those allies makes little military sense.[18] For example, the Obama administration's decision to retire a nuclear variant of the Tomahawk land-attack cruise missile in 2010 raised concerns about the credibility of the U.S. nuclear umbrella over Japan. According to Terence Roehrig of the U.S. Naval War College: "While Tokyo has long been an advocate for denuclearization, the [missile], according to one Japanese analyst, is an important capability *that is a crucial symbol of U.S. credibility.* A U.S. analyst maintained that Japan saw the [missile] as 'their weapon,' providing a tangible capability below strategic nuclear weapons that could be used to retaliate in the event of a nuclear strike."[19] A nuclear arsenal with a wide variety of capabilities is thus an important totem of Washington's commitment to allies writ large.

Nuclear weapons are poised to enjoy a prominent place in U.S. military strategy going forward as Washington focuses on countering other great powers. All of the Trump administration's major strategy documents name Russia and China as America's primary competitors. Senior U.S. officials frequently justify new military capabilities, including new U.S. nuclear weapons, as necessary responses to Russian and Chinese capabilities and activities.[20] Renewed focus on great-power competition has also drawn U.S. attention to nuclear developments in both competitors. As the 2018 NPR states: "While the United States has continued to reduce the number and salience of nuclear weapons . . . Russia and China have moved in the opposite direction. Russia has expanded and improved its strategic and non-strategic nuclear forces. China's military modernization has resulted in an expanded nuclear force, with little to no transparency into its intentions."[21] To counteract these developments, the 2018 NPR increases the relative importance of nuclear weapons in U.S. strategy by, among other things, calling for two new capabilities: a low-yield warhead for the Trident missile and a nuclear-capable, sea-launched cruise missile.[22]

Judged against the criteria of seizing escalation dominance and reassuring allies, the Trump administration's call for new low-yield nuclear weapons and the general elevation of nuclear weapons in U.S. strategy seem appropriate steps for preserving extended deterrence. However, this approach overlooks the specific adversary actions that the United States is trying to deter. This oversight is important. Nuclear weapons are not "one-size-fits-all"; in some scenarios nuclear weapons can be very effective at shaping a target's cost–benefit calculus and decisions, while in other scenarios they are simply not salient.[23] If nuclear weapons are not well suited for deterring Russian and Chinese actions, then elevating their role in U.S. strategy and adding new kinds of weapons to the force structure may not produce the benefits that U.S. leaders expect.

Unlike the Cold War, when the United States was trying to deter a large-scale invasion of western Europe, the primary military threat posed by other great powers today is limited attacks or coercive actions against weaker states to get them to make various concessions. The balance of interests adds another wrinkle as geographic proximity gives potential adversaries a stronger implicit stake in potential conflicts, which could make them more willing than the United States to tolerate risks.[24] Finally, both Russia and China possess secure second-strike nuclear forces that would be very difficult for the United States to eliminate.[25] Any limited U.S. nuclear escalation could be countered by these retaliatory forces, thus making threats of limited nuclear escalation by the United States less credible. U.S. nuclear weapons, regardless of their yield, could have difficulty deterring a conventional attack in scenarios where the scale of conflict appears limited, adversary interests are strong, and the adversary has a secure second-strike capability.

If general deterrence were to break down, the chief problem facing the United States would be keeping a conventional conflict from turning into a nuclear one. American war plans are classified, but they would most likely involve deep strikes against Russian and Chinese air defenses, command and control nodes, and logistics facilities to destroy the latter's "anti-access/area denial" (A2/AD) zones.[26] Such attacks create ample opportunity for inadvertent nuclear escalation, especially if the target fears that its ability to conduct nuclear retaliation is disrupted in the process.[27] Additionally, Russia and China would have a strong incentive to target U.S. satellites and radar installations because these systems enable conventional operations.[28] However, the United States also depends on these assets to conduct nuclear attack and missile defense operations, so attacks against these assets could have the unintentional effect of degrading America's ability to use its nuclear weapons effectively. A flexible U.S. nuclear arsenal would most likely not deter these kinds of attacks if adversaries are conducting them with the intent of disrupting U.S. conventional forces.

If the value of nuclear weapons for deterring limited conventional conflict and controlling escalation within such a conflict is questionable, then they have practically no bearing on the more common, less intense forms of great-power competition that the United States wants to prevent. For example, both Russia and China have actively challenged the United States in cyberspace, the former trying to influence U.S. elections and the latter stealing troves of government and private-sector information.[29] China's construction of artificial islands in the South China Sea raises alarm bells in Washington about Beijing's ability to limit the U.S. military's freedom of operation in the western Pacific and concern about China's long-term intentions.[30] Deterring these and other forms of low-level competition is probably impossible for the United States. Indeed, Russia and China take such actions precisely because they can achieve their objectives with little risk of further escalation. Dealing with these common, low-intensity forms of competition requires greater investment in the diplomatic, intelligence, and economic instruments of U.S. power, not nuclear weapons.

Adding new low-yield nuclear strike capabilities to the U.S. arsenal and increasing the prominence of nuclear weapons in U.S. strategy are typical reactions for policymakers contending with great-power rivals that challenge long-standing extended deterrence commitments.

Such an approach worked well during the last period of such competition, so why not reach for similar solutions today? However, while nuclear weapons are valuable for deterring nuclear attacks against the United States and its allies, their ability to prevent limited conventional attacks or coercion is questionable at best. So long as Washington remains committed to extended deterrence, it should find ways to buttress its commitments that do not rely on nuclear weapons.

A Different Approach to Deterring Great Powers

At its core, deterrence is about preventing an adversary from taking an unwanted action (such as attacking an ally) by issuing credible threats to inflict unacceptable costs if it does. Deterrence is frequently associated with nuclear weapons because of their ability to quickly inflict astounding levels of destruction upon a target.[31] However, while nuclear weapons are important components of a deterrent strategy, they are not the only tool that states can use to impose costs on an adversary.

Modern precision-guided conventional weapons and short-range missile defenses make warfare defense dominant now and for the foreseeable future; it is much costlier for an aggressor state to take an aggressive action than it is for the defender to protect itself.[32] Conventional capabilities can't match the raw destructive power of nuclear weapons, but they have some advantages over nuclear weapons for both preconflict deterrence and controlling escalation should a conflict occur.[33] Nuclear weapons are still an important component of extended deterrence, but their relative value is decreasing as defensively focused conventional capabilities improve.[34] American policymakers should place greater emphasis on the nonnuclear contributors to extended deterrence.

As stated earlier in this chapter, the principal scenario that the United States is trying to prevent is limited, regional conflict between great-power adversaries and U.S. allies. The chief advantage that nonnuclear systems have over nuclear weapons for deterring this kind of conflict stems from their usability. While it is innately believable that the United States would use nuclear weapons to protect itself from attack, it is much less believable that Washington would use them to protect its allies, especially if the country threatening the U.S. ally could absorb a U.S. nuclear strike and retaliate in kind. As the late Thomas Schelling, author of the path-breaking nuclear deterrence book *Arms and Influence*, put it, "The difference between the national homeland and everything 'abroad' is the difference between threats that are inherently credible . . . and threats that have to be made credible."[35]

Conventional weapons, by contrast, do not have a credibility problem. States want to preserve their territorial integrity and protect their populations, and they will fight to defend themselves from aggression, even in the face of overwhelming odds.[36] What conventional weapons lack in raw destructive power compared with nuclear weapons, they make up for with inherent credibility; the virtual guarantee that conventional weapons would be used in a conflict means that the aggressor must always take them into account. Nuclear weapons, by contrast, may not affect an aggressor's risk–reward calculus if it believes it can control the scope of a conflict and has a stronger stake in the outcome than the United States because of political interest or geographic proximity. For example, if China wants to use military force to seize control of Taiwan, it must factor into its planning the conventional assets of both Taiwan and the United States. However, Chinese leaders may discount the likelihood of the United States using nuclear weapons to defend Taiwan, given Beijing's ability to respond to U.S. nuclear use with its own nuclear forces. China's strong political interest in controlling Taiwan, coupled with its improved conventional capabilities and secure nuclear retaliatory force, could cause its leaders to assume that any hypothetical U.S. nuclear threat would not be credible.[37]

Nonnuclear capabilities also have advantages for preventing inadvertent nuclear escalation within a conflict should general deterrence fail—but only if the United States rethinks its general military strategy toward great-power rivals. A common feature of Chinese and Russian military strategy is the emphasis placed on denying the United States the ability to project military power, especially air power, in the areas close to each country's borders—the A2/AD strategy mentioned earlier. America's counter-A2/AD strategy most likely involves attacks against the capabilities that enable A2/AD, including command and control facilities, early-warning sensors, communications networks, and military bases, deep within Russian and Chinese territory.[38] Beijing and Moscow would likely prioritize destroying similar U.S. assets to prevent the United States from obtaining the situational awareness necessary to conduct an effective counter-A2/AD campaign.[39] However, many of these systems are dual-use, meaning that they have a role in carrying out nuclear as well as conventional military operations. Attacks against these dual-use systems intended to be part of a conventional, counter-A2/AD campaign could be perceived either as a prelude to nuclear strikes or as an attempt to degrade the target's ability to defend itself with nuclear weapons, thus increasing the risk of inadvertent nuclear escalation.[40]

The United States can reduce these inadvertent escalation risks by giving greater responsibility to frontline allies for blunting an adversary's offensive push. Because of geography, the United States must play an "away game" when it fights other great powers, which is why Washington needs to go after enemy A2/AD zones quickly in a conflict. America's allies don't have to think about conflict in the same way. Instead of having militaries that emphasize power projection, allies ought to focus on creating their own A2/AD zones that use a mix of relatively low-cost conventional strike capabilities and missile defenses to bog down any attempts to attack and seize disputed territory.[41] Allied states probably will not be able to defeat the conventional forces of Russia and China, but they can still impose costs and prevent the attacker from achieving a quick and decisive victory.[42]

Stronger allies capable of holding their own would take pressure off the United States to rapidly implement a counter-A2/AD strategy and therefore reduce the associated inadvertent escalation risks. Additionally, the attacking country would still have to weigh the risks of eventual U.S. intervention. Inadvertent escalation would still be possible in this scenario—eliminating that risk is impossible—but the relative risk of the conventional conflict going nuclear would be significantly lower. Furthermore, better-armed allies would have more options available to them for detecting and resisting hostile great-power actions that fall below the threshold of armed conflict.

Conclusion

The desire to maintain extended deterrence commitments is an important driver of U.S. nuclear strategy and force structure decisions. Washington is understandably concerned about recent military developments in Russia and China and believes that nuclear weapons will be an important tool in this new period of great-power competition. However, nuclear weapons are not a silver bullet. They may not be the most effective means for either deterring the kinds of conflict most likely to bring the United States to blows with Russia and China or controlling escalation should general deterrence fail.

Instead of forging ahead with the wide-ranging and expensive nuclear modernization effort conceived by the Obama administration or the new, low-yield nuclear capabilities proposed by the Trump administration, U.S. policymakers should consider the other capabilities that can deter adversaries and control escalation within conflict. Alternative combinations of capabilities and military strategies can meet Washington's strategic goals of protecting allies and making aggression prohibitively costly without the significant changes to U.S. nuclear force structure currently under consideration. A military strategy that emphasizes stronger frontline allies using conventional capabilities to create their own A2/AD zones is a credible way to deter aggression by other great powers and at the same time reduces the risk of inadvertent nuclear escalation.

7. Nuclear Blackmail

The Threat from North Korea and Iran

Matthew Fuhrmann and Todd S. Sechser

In October 2006, the Democratic People's Republic of Korea (DPRK) conducted its first successful test of a nuclear device. In U.S. foreign policy circles, the conversation about North Korea's nuclear program underwent a marked shift. Having focused for more than a decade on preventing North Korea from acquiring a nuclear arsenal, the policy debate began to center around the consequences of having failed to achieve that objective. Now that North Korea had crossed the nuclear threshold, how would it use its newfound capability?

This question has become even more pressing as North Korea's nuclear capabilities have grown. In September 2017, North Korea conducted its sixth and largest nuclear test, which it claimed to be a thermonuclear device. U.S. intelligence agencies have estimated that North Korea has enough fissile material for between 30 and 60 nuclear warheads.[1] As its nuclear capabilities have expanded, so too has North Korea's ability to deliver nuclear weapons to faraway targets. Under Kim Jong Un's leadership, North Korea has conducted more than 80 missile tests, including a test of a missile that could place the entire continental United States within the range of North Korean nuclear forces.[2]

What will North Korea try to do with its nuclear weapons? It is widely believed that at least one purpose of North Korea's nuclear arsenal is to deter an attack from the United States and protect the survival of the Kim regime. For their part, North Korean officials have long held that self-defense is the primary motivation for the country's nuclear program, asserting that "nuclear weapons will help DPRK avoid the fate of Iraq, Afghanistan, Libya, and Syria."[3]

But many observers believe that North Korea's objectives are much more ambitious. They argue that its aims are offensive, not defensive, and that it plans to use nuclear threats to fracture U.S. alliances with South Korea and Japan, to undermine the U.S. military presence in East Asia, and even to forcibly reunify the Korean peninsula under North Korean control.[4] During his tenure as director of the Central Intelligence Agency, for example, current Secretary of State Mike Pompeo argued that North Korea's nuclear weapons were meant for "more than just regime preservation . . . coercive is perhaps the best way to think about how Kim Jong Un is prepared to potentially use these weapons."[5] In this view, North Korea's nuclear arsenal gives it the ability to practice coercion and blackmail, not just deterrence.

Recent debates about Iran feature similar arguments. Iran does not possess nuclear weapons, but the growth of its uranium enrichment capability over the past decade fostered anxious speculation about how Iran might behave as a nuclear power. Would it simply seek to deter its adversaries or instead attempt to intimidate and blackmail them into making concessions? Many observers fear the latter. One Arab official reportedly put it this way: "What happens after Iran gets a nuclear bomb? The next day they will tell the king of Bahrain to hand over power to the opposition. They will tell Qatar to send the American Air Force home. And they will tell King Abdullah [of Saudi Arabia], 'This is how much oil you may pump and this is what the price of oil will now be.'"[6] A former high-ranking official in the U.S. Department of Defense argued along similar lines: "A nuclear Iran would be disastrous for the countries of the region and for the United States. . . . The Islamic Republic could be emboldened to act even more aggressively than it currently does in regional or global conflicts. . . . Iran would extraordinarily increase its coercive leverage."[7]

These pessimistic projections reflect a broader view about the role nuclear weapons play in international relations. During the Cold War, most discussions about nuclear weapons in U.S. foreign policy revolved around deterrence. But protecting the United States and its allies is just one half of the equation. Nuclear weapons might also help countries commit aggression, not just prevent it. By threatening nuclear attack, nuclear-armed states might be able to pressure adversaries into giving up territory, changing their foreign policy, deposing a leader, or making other kinds of concessions. In other words, nuclear weapons might be useful instruments of *coercion*—for changing the status quo.

Scholars and policymakers often argue that nuclear weapons are effective weapons of coercion, not just deterrence. This "coercionist school" of nuclear politics holds that the threat of nuclear punishment can induce states not only to refrain from aggression, but also to make concessions they would not otherwise make. As political scientist Robert Pape has argued, "Even if the coercer's nuclear resources are limited, the prospect of damage far worse than the most intense conventional assault will likely coerce all but the most resolute defenders."[8] The idea is simple: no state wants to suffer the terrifyingly destructive consequences of a nuclear attack. When confronted with a coercive demand backed by the threat of nuclear punishment, a leader has no choice but to back down, even if it means relinquishing something valuable.

The coercionist school has a long lineage in American foreign policy. At the very outset of the nuclear age, U.S. officials expressed optimism that the U.S. nuclear monopoly would allow it to bully the Soviets into accepting America's vision for the postwar world: "After all, we've got [the atomic bomb] and they haven't," boasted Harry Truman's secretary of state, James Byrnes.[9] This belief has also underpinned fears about nuclear proliferation: in the 1960s, for example, U.S. officials worried that China's imminent acquisition of nuclear weapons would aid its efforts to "eject the United States from Asia" through coercion and intimidation.[10]

The policy implications of this perspective are stark: if nuclear weapons are indeed useful tools of coercion, then nuclear proliferation is not merely a threat to international stability—it is a threat to America's position in the world. North Korea might be emboldened to make "even greater demands and coercive nuclear threats," and a nuclear Iran could become "the dominant regional power in the Middle East," able to compel its adversaries to do its bidding.[11] Military action might be justified to avert these outcomes—as many have advocated.[12]

How well does the historical record support these views? Can new nuclear states more effectively impose their will on adversaries, either by threat or by force? In this chapter, we argue that the coercionist view suffers from several logical and historical errors. Coercive nuclear threats face a nearly insurmountable credibility problem that stems from the fundamental distinction between deterrence and "compellence." A close look at the evidence supports this view, suggesting that worst-case fears about nuclear coercion from North Korea and Iran are not warranted.

Compellence and the Nuclear Credibility Gap

"The aggressor is always peace-loving," wrote the Prussian military theorist Carl von Clausewitz. "He would prefer to take over our country unopposed."[13] Clausewitz's insight reminds us that coercion is most successful when military force is not used at all: winning without a fight is the coercer's ideal outcome.

Thomas Schelling coined the term "compellence" to describe threats aimed at changing the status quo.[14] Compellent threats are distinct from deterrent threats, which aim to prevent an adversary from taking action. Demands to relinquish territory, to withdraw troops, to change national policies, or to abdicate from power all fall under the umbrella of compellence. Is North Korea—or, perhaps someday, Iran—better positioned to make compellent threats because of its nuclear capability?

In our book *Nuclear Weapons and Coercive Diplomacy*, we evaluated the coercionist school's assertion that compellent threats are more effective when they are made by countries wielding nuclear weapons.[15] We used a comprehensive database of more than 200 compellent threats to determine whether nuclear-armed coercers achieve their goals more often without resorting to war.[16] The database contains well-known cases of attempted compellence (e.g., U.S. threats during the Cuban missile crisis), as well as more obscure episodes. Moreover, it contains threats made by both nuclear and nonnuclear coercers. By comparing their success rates, we sought to reveal the utility—or futility—of nuclear coercion.

The evidence suggests that nuclear weapons offer few advantages for coercers hoping to use threats to alter the status quo. Three patterns stand out. First, compellent threats are not more successful when they are made by nuclear powers: in the database of compellent threats, roughly 20 percent of threats from nuclear states succeeded, compared with 32 percent from nonnuclear states.[17] Second, having nuclear superiority does not improve the effectiveness of compellent threats: indeed, every compellent threat issued by a nuclear-armed state was issued against a state that had either an inferior nuclear arsenal or none at all.[18] Third, targeting adversaries that lack the ability to retaliate with nuclear weapons does not improve the odds of success: nuclear coercers compiled just a 16 percent success rate against nonnuclear adversaries, while other types of threats clocked in at 33 percent. This evidence is not encouraging for North Korean or Iranian officials who believe that nuclear weapons will give them a trump card to wield against recalcitrant neighbors.[19]

Why are nuclear weapons such poor tools of compellence? Answering this question requires understanding how compellence differs from its counterpart, deterrence. Deterrent threats are often credible because they aim to protect what a nation already owns. Not only are the stakes often very high in deterrence—rising even perhaps to the level of national survival—but the secondary political costs of using nuclear weapons for deterrence are minimal, since self-defense is widely seen as a legitimate justification for using extreme military measures. No mental gymnastics are needed to imagine, for example, that North Korea or a nuclear Iran would be willing to use nuclear weapons to repel an invader.

Compellent threats, however, are different. Because they aim to alter the status quo, compellent threats necessarily center around objects or issues that the coercer covets but does not possess—and may never have possessed. In other words, the coercer has already demonstrated that it can live without its demands being met, even if it would prefer not to. This fact might not be problematic if the costs of using nuclear weapons for compellence were minimal. However, they are not likely to be. Using nuclear threats—to say nothing of actual nuclear strikes—to extract concessions from an adversary would entail significant drawbacks for would-be coercers. A nuclear coercer could find itself isolated, targeted by crippling international sanctions, or even subject to attack by a coalition that feared becoming its next victim.[20] In short, states face higher costs and lower stakes when practicing nuclear coercion compared to nuclear deterrence. Both weaken the credibility of coercive nuclear threats.

This logic calls into question the intrinsic credibility of a coercive nuclear threat from North Korea or Iran. One could envision a scenario in which North Korea demanded that South Korea stop hosting U.S. troops, while making thinly veiled references to its nuclear arsenal to underscore the threat. Were Iran to acquire nuclear weapons in the future, perhaps it could demand something similar of its neighbors. Yet it would be difficult to believe these threats. Simply issuing them—much less carrying them out—would drive countries deeper into the arms of the United States, other regional powers, and one another. North Korea and Iran would find themselves more isolated and their adversaries more unified. Given that both countries have been able to live with U.S. troops nearby for decades, their avowal that they had suddenly, precipitously reached a breaking point that made them willing to suffer dire costs to evict U.S. forces from their respective neighborhoods would be difficult to believe.

In nuclear confrontations, credibility is both essential and elusive. The historical record demonstrates that using nuclear weapons to deter aggression is easier than using them to engage in it. Even if North Korean or Iranian leaders are emboldened to try to overturn the status quo with coercive threats, nuclear weapons are unlikely to play a role in their success or failure.

Nuclear Shields and Territorial Aggression

The preceding discussion underscores the likelihood that explicit attempts at nuclear blackmail will fail. However, nuclear powers might be able to impose their will on other countries in a subtler way—one that does not involve verbal ultimatums. A revisionist state armed with nuclear weapons could seize a slice of disputed territory without warning and force its adversary to fight in order to reverse the aggressor's gains. Fighting would be risky, based on this line of thinking, because it could lead to nuclear escalation. Having nuclear weapons, then, might enable countries to engage in territorial aggression with greater ease.

Are nuclear arsenals akin to large shields that protect countries from retaliation following aggressive maneuvers? We examined the connection between nuclear arsenals and territorial aggression in *Nuclear Weapons and Coercive Diplomacy*. Using a database that contains information on 348 territorial disputes in the 20th century—including prominent cases like the Kashmir conflict between India and Pakistan—we studied the history of nuclear-backed aggression.[21] Our approach was simple: we looked at whether nuclear powers behaved differently or experienced more favorable outcomes than their nonnuclear counterparts when relying on military force to settle territorial disputes. We found that they did not. In general, concerns about nuclear weapons facilitating territorial faits accomplis are overblown.

First, nuclear-armed countries and nonnuclear states initiate military challenges over territory at a similar rate. For both groups, fighting occurs in 6 percent of the relevant opportunities. Nuclear powers do sometimes use military force in an attempt to overturn the status quo. For example, the Soviet Union provoked a confrontation with the United States and its allies over the status of Berlin from 1958 to 1961. And Russia challenged Georgia militarily during a dispute over military basing rights in the 1990s. But nonnuclear states fight over territory with the same frequency, suggesting that nuclear weapons do not generate unique emboldening effects.

Second, nuclear weapons do not appear to embolden countries to engage in conventional escalation during ongoing military conflicts. The nuclear coercionist school implies that countries will push harder during confrontations when they have a nuclear advantage, but history tells a different story. In our database, nuclear-armed challengers escalated disputes in just 4 of their 21 opportunities to do so. Those four episodes all occurred in the context of a single case: China's border dispute with Vietnam. Nonnuclear challengers actually escalated at a slightly higher rate (24 percent compared to 19 percent).

Third, nuclear powers rarely succeed when they use military force in an attempt to redraw the map. We examined the outcomes of all cases in our database in which nuclear-armed challengers instigated military disputes. There were 23 such episodes of conflict across 7 territorial disputes. Our analysis reveals that 70 percent of the time, military force failed to produce major territorial gains for the nuclear power. Proponents of the "nuclear shield" argument often point to Pakistan as a case that illustrates the utility of nuclear weapons for territorial aggression.[22] Pakistan has indeed instigated military challenges in the context of the Kashmir dispute, but it has little to show for its efforts. Islamabad's 1999 gambit to surreptitiously seize land in the mountainous Kargil region of Kashmir, for instance, did not result in any territorial gains.

These findings carry lessons for contemporary policy debates. U.S. officials on both sides of the aisle worry that Iran would use nuclear weapons as a shield for aggression if it were to obtain an arsenal. For example, Colin Kahl, who served as deputy assistant to the U.S. president and national security advisor to the vice president from 2014 to 2017, wrote in 2012 that if Iran had nuclear weapons, "Tehran would likely dial up its trouble-making and capitalize on its deterrent to limit the response options available to threatened states."[23] Robert Danin, a scholar at the Council on Foreign Relations, expressed similar fears, arguing that "Iran's nuclear capability could lead it to use its conventional military forces more aggressively."[24] These concerns have some merit. However, the possibility of Iran engaging in nuclear-backed aggression is less threatening than it might initially appear.

The "nuclear shield" argument assumes that getting nuclear weapons emboldens states to do things that they otherwise would not. However, nuclear and nonnuclear states tend to behave similarly, at least in the case of territorial aggression. Proponents of the view that nuclear weapons embolden aggression often point to actions Iran might take if it gets a nuclear bomb—for example, supporting Shiite extremist groups such as Hezbollah or threatening to escalate territorial disputes with neighboring countries.[25] But Tehran is already doing these things as a nonnuclear state. It is far from obvious that getting nuclear weapons would lead to an overall increase in Iranian aggression, as opposed to continuation of its present policies.

This brings us to the question of effectiveness. Could Iran alter the status quo in its favor through nuclear-backed faits accomplis? Our analysis suggests that it could not. Other revisionist leaders have had little luck using threats of nuclear retaliation to swipe territory or other valuable objects from their adversaries. It is hard to see why Iran would fare better.

The Soviet experience offers a valuable illustration. In 1962, Nikita Khrushchev introduced nuclear missiles in Cuba. He intended to present the United States with a fait accompli. As Khrushchev instructed the Presidium: "Carry this out secretly. Then declare it."[26] Once these capabilities were revealed, the United States would face a stark choice: accept the new status quo or use military force to reverse it. Khrushchev seemingly believed that his nuclear arsenal would compel Washington to choose the former course. Unfortunately for Khrushchev, his operation did not go according to plan. His actions triggered the Cuban Missile Crisis, which brought the two superpowers to the brink of nuclear war. Khrushchev ultimately caved to the U.S. demand to remove the missiles from the island.[27] These events underscore the point that nuclear-backed aggression can be exceedingly dangerous and does not ultimately benefit those who attempt it.

Timing matters when it comes to nuclear-backed aggression. A 2009 study by the political scientist Michael Horowitz shows that nuclear powers behave more aggressively than nonnuclear states—but only in the first few years after they acquire an arsenal.[28] A nuclear-armed Iran might well follow this pattern. Tehran might attempt to employ its arsenal as a shield shortly after becoming a nuclear power. For example, it might fuel Hezbollah-backed attacks against Israel or escalate its involvement in the Syrian civil war. Over time, though, Iran is likely to learn a valuable lesson: nuclear-backed faits accomplis do not pay off. The United States could facilitate the learning process by frustrating Tehran's initial attempts to gain ground via nuclear shield–backed aggression—if it were to attempt such ploys.

Nuclear Coercion and Preventive War

The preceding analysis carries implications for U.S. nonproliferation policy. It may help officials better understand the options that they should (or should not) pursue to counter the international spread of nuclear weapons.

One option in the nonproliferation toolkit is preventive strikes against an adversary's nuclear facilities. The goal of this policy is to eliminate critical infrastructure, thereby eroding a state's capacity to make bombs. This option has a rich history. Countries have seriously considered attacking enemies' nuclear plants no fewer than 18 times.[29] Some of these cases resulted in actual preventive strikes. Israel, for instance, carried out two prominent attacks in the name of nonproliferation—one against Iraq in 1981 and another that targeted Syria in 2007. Preventive strikes are a potential option for dealing with the nuclear challenges posed by Iran and North Korea today. There are signs that President Donald Trump once favored (and may still desire) such an approach.

President Trump withdrew from the nonproliferation agreement with Iran known as the Joint Comprehensive Plan of Action on May 8, 2018. This move led to speculation about the possible use of military force against Tehran. John Bolton, Trump's current national security advisor, has been a vocal proponent of this option. His 2015 op-ed in the *New York Times* had the title "To Stop Iran's Bomb, Bomb Iran."[30] Trump himself has hinted at the possibility of attacking Iran. He threatened Iranian president Hassan Rouhani in a July 22, 2018, tweet: "NEVER, EVER THREATEN THE UNITED STATES AGAIN OR YOU WILL SUFFER CONSEQUENCES THE LIKES OF WHICH FEW THROUGHOUT HISTORY HAVE EVER SUFFERED BEFORE."[31]

Trump has similarly raised the prospect of war with North Korea. In August 2017, he threatened to unleash "fire and fury like the world has never seen" against Pyongyang.[32] Ten months later, he met with North Korean leader Kim Jong Un in Singapore during a historic summit. The two leaders released a statement shortly after their meeting in which Pyongyang pledged to "work toward complete denuclearization of the Korean peninsula."[33] Yet many people doubt that North Korea will give up its nuclear weapons. After all, the Singapore declaration represents a vague, open-ended commitment—not an ironclad promise to unilaterally disarm, as some people interpret it. Trump is reportedly frustrated by North Korea's lack of progress on disarmament.[34] The prospect of military force looms in the background if North Korea continues to dig in its heels.

Advocates of preventive strikes often accept the nuclear coercionist take on blackmail. A nuclear-armed Iran or North Korea, they argue, can bully the world into submission. In an article titled "The Case for Bombing Iran," one observer argued that an Iranian nuclear capability would allow it to "dominate the greater Middle East, and thereby to control the oilfields of the region and the flow of oil out of it through the Persian Gulf," simply through the use of "intimidation and blackmail."[35] The only way to avoid being victimized by Iran, advocates of preventive war argue, is to attack its nuclear facilities before it's too late.

If nuclear weapons enable aggression and victimization—not merely self-defense—preventive strikes against nuclear programs may be warranted in some situations. Our analysis shows, however, that they generally do not. This finding substantially weakens the argument in favor of military strikes against Iran or North Korea.[36] There are, in fact, many undesirable effects associated with nuclear proliferation. For instance, the further spread of nuclear weapons increases the risk that nuclear weapons will be used because of accidents or miscalculation. But worst-case thinking about contemporary proliferators is badly misguided and potentially dangerous.

Conclusion

The fear of nuclear blackmail permeates international politics. World leaders worry that their adversaries will bully them into submission by dangling nuclear threats. They also fear that a nuclear-armed rival could use its arsenal to commit aggression with greater ease. Both of these concerns are largely unfounded. Nuclear weapons have great utility in some situations—particularly in defending the homeland against invasions. But they are poorly suited for changing the status quo. Coercive nuclear threats lack credibility because they would be too costly for the coercer to implement in most situations. There is little evidence that nuclear powers are systematically more aggressive than their non-nuclear counterparts. When nuclear-armed countries have attempted daring land grabs or other faits accomplis, they have often failed.

Nuclear proliferation is by no means desirable for the United States. Officials in Washington would do well to consider the coercive limitations of nuclear weapons when crafting U.S. nonproliferation policies. In many circumstances, when attempting to influence the behavior of nascent nuclear-weapons states or the decisionmaking of states that are contemplating joining the nuclear club, it may be wiser to reach for diplomatic and economic tools than military ones.

8. Preserving the U.S. Arms Control Legacy in the Trump Era

Maggie Tennis

The Trump administration's decision to withdraw from the Joint Comprehensive Plan of Action (JCPOA) with Iran and the Intermediate-Range Nuclear Forces (INF) Treaty with Russia and its delay in negotiating an extension of the New Strategic Arms Reduction Treaty (New START) jeopardize America's long-held position as an arms control leader. The current administration's position on all three agreements demonstrates a troubling trend that devalues diplomacy.[1]

This chapter examines the consequences of these departures in a challenging security and political environment. The suspension of U.S. participation in the Iran deal and the collapse of the INF Treaty will damage relations with U.S. allies and could trigger arms races in the Middle East, Asia, and even Europe. In addition, these moves threaten the existence of New START by exacerbating tensions with Russia and demonstrating a declining interest in arms control writ large. However, New START may prove robust enough to withstand both waning administration support for arms control and a general downturn in U.S.–Russia relations. Extending the treaty would maintain its significant restrictions and transparency measures while signaling that the United States remains committed to some degree of arms control.

The Joint Comprehensive Plan of Action

The JCPOA is an agreement between Iran, the European Union (EU), and the P5+1 (the five permanent members of the United Nations [UN] Security Council—China, France, Russia, the United Kingdom, and the United States—plus Germany). It constrains Iran's ability to produce fissile material and, by extension, nuclear weapons.[2] Per the agreement,

Iran placed limits on the number and type of centrifuges it operates, restricted its uranium enrichment activities, and redesigned the Arak heavy water reactor. Iran's leadership also agreed to more intrusive and frequent monitoring and inspections of its nuclear facilities than were previously in place from Iran's membership in the International Atomic Energy Agency (IAEA) and the Treaty on the Non-Proliferation of Nuclear Weapons (NPT). In January 2016, the IAEA confirmed that Iran had taken the initial steps required to trigger relief from American, EU, and UN sanctions.[3] According to the planned timeline, if Iran demonstrated consistent compliance with the deal's limitations and monitoring and verification measures by October 2023, the UN would suspend its restrictions on Iranian ballistic missiles, the EU would eliminate its remaining sanctions, and the United States would eliminate some remaining sanctions and remove certain entities from sanctions lists.

That timeline was disrupted in May 2018 when President Donald Trump announced he would withdraw the United States from the JCPOA and reinstate U.S. sanctions on Iran.[4] Two waves of sanctions entered into effect in 2018: an initial wave in August followed by restrictions on Iran's oil and financial sectors in November.[5]

Like any negotiated compromise, the JCPOA is an imperfect deal. Although it limited Iran's ability to produce material for a nuclear weapon, it did not permanently block that ability, nor did it confront other security challenges presented by Iran. For example, the deal did not address Iran's ballistic missile program, and the accompanying UN Security Council resolution relaxed conventional arms and missile embargoes. Opponents of the deal argued that, by loosening pressure on Iran's economy, the JCPOA enabled Iran to expand its malign behavior in the Middle East, particularly its support for terrorist groups such as Hezbollah.[6] These flaws turned most American conservatives, and the Trump administration, against the deal.

However, the U.S. decision to leave the JCPOA and reinstate sanctions threatens to upend the agreement's significant accomplishments, including unprecedented concessions by the Iranians. Both the IAEA and the U.S. State Department had confirmed Iran's compliance with the JCPOA's terms.[7] In January 2019, leaders of the U.S. intelligence community testified to the Senate that Iran has continued to implement the JCPOA.[8] Since the deal was signed, 98 percent of Iran's low-enriched uranium has been shipped abroad, the Arak heavy water reactor was rendered effectively nonfunctional, and the IAEA was given access to supervise Iran's remaining nuclear facilities.[9] The deal provided critical insight into Iran's nuclear activities through comprehensive verification and transparency mechanisms. And, perhaps most significantly, the deal reduced any possible foreign policy leverage that Iran might have obtained were it to possess a nuclear deterrent. The JCPOA successfully precluded Iran from becoming the world's 10th nuclear weapons state.

Finally, by demonstrating how a coalition approach could combat a potential regional nuclear threat, the JCPOA paved the way for future similar efforts. In fact, the coalition-led nature of the agreement might allow it to survive despite U.S. withdrawal because its terms enable other parties to continue providing sanctions relief. Britain, France, Germany, the EU, Russia, and China intend to continue their adherence to the deal as well as their business relationships with Iran.[10]

By exiting the JCPOA, the Trump administration has sacrificed numerous advantages of the deal: insight into Iran's nuclear program; leverage with Tehran; and the formal and informal channels of communication that the deal facilitated. U.S. withdrawal is a major blow to America's European allies, especially the P5+1 countries that spent weeks warning the White House against leaving the deal. As a result, Washington may lose international support for initiatives aimed at countering other Iranian activities in the region, including transfers of Iranian weapons technology and expertise to other countries and non-state actors.[11] Furthermore, allies may view the move as a rejection of coalition-led nonproliferation. In any event, the decision undermines Washington's historic position as a partner to Europe and as a leader of arms control and nonproliferation. States such as North Korea may have less reason to trust Washington's involvement in future nonproliferation negotiations or commitments.[12]

Moreover, the U.S. decision might provide an opportunity for Iran to restart efforts to develop a nuclear capability—or prompt Iran to withdraw from the agreement altogether. Iran could try to gain back the international leverage it enjoyed before the deal as a near-nuclear state, likely by seeking the technology integral to nuclear bomb material development. In fact, the head of Iran's Atomic Energy Organization announced the completion of a facility that would allow Iran to develop and assemble centrifuges that are used to enrich uranium.[13] Although these centrifuges are technically permitted under the JCPOA, a renewed effort to acquire them is troubling in light of Supreme Leader Ayatollah Ali Khamenei's declaration that Iran will increase its uranium enrichment capacity if the JCPOA falls apart.[14] The prospect of Iran ramping up enrichment capabilities could further destabilize the Middle East if other countries are goaded into either pursuing their own nuclear capabilities or engaging in preemptive attacks against Iran.[15]

Policy Recommendations

Following the announcement that the United States would leave the JCPOA, Iran's Ayatollah Khamenei said Iran would remain in the deal if other members continue purchasing Iranian oil and do not support Washington's call to limit Iran's ballistic missile program.[16] Meanwhile, Secretary of State Mike Pompeo called for increasing pressure on Iran and laid out 12 demands for negotiating a new deal on Washington's terms.[17] Most of these demands are infeasible because they violate key Iranian interests—even the country's core sovereign rights. Acquiescing could turn domestic public opinion against Tehran. Nevertheless, the Trump administration appears set on its strategy. A recent article by Pompeo describes the administration's strategy as "squeezing" Iran through sanctions and includes language indicating a long-term desire for regime change.[18] This path is unlikely to be successful, due to a lack of international support for renewed sanctions and Tehran's ability to stoke anti-American sentiment among the Iranian people through propaganda. Moreover, American threats of regime change will likely make Iranian hardliners more intransigent.[19]

The White House seems to be playing a waiting game that is growing more provocative, given a recent U.S. decision to deploy a carrier strike group and bomber task force to the Persian Gulf. But the more constructive—and controllable—option is to identify a combination of incentives and disincentives to pressure Iran not to restart its nuclear program. Because the JCPOA remains the best foundation for curbing Iran's nuclear activities, the ideal course is to rejoin the agreement, with modifications, when political circumstances allow. This path would require Iran to remain a party to the deal in the interim and to agree to negotiate modifications and a follow-on arrangement in good faith.

With this goal in mind, officials and experts from the U.S. nongovernmental community should focus on repairing damaged alliance relationships between the United States and the European members of the JCPOA and strengthening efforts to sustain Iranian compliance with the deal. First, they should discourage the White House from enforcing secondary sanctions on European countries that do business in Iran.[20] Iran is more likely to withdraw from the deal if it cannot rely on European economic partners. Indeed, Iranian officials have said they will determine whether to stay in the deal after evaluating a European economic package meant to mitigate the effect of U.S. sanctions.[21] Hassan Rouhani, Iran's president, has declared that Iran will continue to meet its JCPOA obligations so long as it enjoys the deal's economic advantages.[22]

At the 2018 UN General Assembly meeting, the EU, China, and Russia announced the creation of a special purpose vehicle (SPV) that is supposed to facilitate trade with Iran despite U.S. sanctions.[23] In January 2019, France, Germany, and the United Kingdom introduced their own SPV, called the Instrument for Supporting Trade Exchanges (INSTEX). The aim of INSTEX is to facilitate trade in critical sectors, including pharmaceuticals and agriculture, by "reducing the need for transactions between the European and Iranian financial systems. It will do this by allowing European exporters to receive payments for sales to Iran from funds that are already within Europe, and vice versa."[24] Although it is unclear how INSTEX will work or how beneficial it will be, especially for larger firms, its creation demonstrates a political commitment by the remaining parties to maintain Iran's participation in the deal. American legislators who favor the deal's survival should support Europe in recognizing and implementing other opportunities to support Iran economically, and they should support non-European country membership in INSTEX—as a symbol if nothing else. They should also encourage the administration to scale back reimposed U.S. sanctions if Iran stays in compliance with the JCPOA.

To safeguard the JCPOA until it is possible for Washington to rejoin the deal, U.S. policymakers must help strengthen the efforts of other signatories to reduce the impact of the Trump administration's sanctions. The coalition-focused nature of the JCPOA may be its saving grace if other members of the deal can keep it alive until the United States changes course.

The Intermediate-Range Nuclear Forces Treaty

The INF Treaty is the latest casualty of diminished support for arms control. Its demise highlights the current administration's neglect of arms control as a tool of nuclear stability. Signed by the Soviet Union and the United States in 1987, the INF Treaty required both countries to eliminate and permanently forswear all nuclear and conventional ground-launched ballistic and cruise missiles with ranges of 500–5,500 kilometers. The two states destroyed nearly 2,700 missiles by May 1991, thereby defusing an arms race in Europe.[25] INF-range missiles are considered destabilizing because their short flight distances reduce warning times of nuclear attack and impede the targeted country's ability to organize a retaliatory strike.[26] By prohibiting these weapons, the INF Treaty advanced strategic stability and brought one dangerous arms race between the United States and Soviet Union under control.

In recent years, however, new weapons technologies and the growth of INF-range capabilities in countries not party to the treaty (e.g., China) made membership in the treaty less appealing for Russia. In late 2007, a high-ranking Russia official told then-Secretary of Defense Robert Gates that Russia wanted to withdraw from the treaty so it could better respond to threats posed by other countries along its periphery.[27] Washington rejected these proposals as well as calls to include other countries in the treaty.[28]

Rather than invoking the clause of the INF Treaty that would allow Russia to unilaterally withdraw from it, Moscow began developing and testing, and later deploying, a prohibited missile system.[29] In 2014, the United States formally accused Russia of testing a noncompliant ground-launched cruise missile (GLCM).[30] The Kremlin then expressed its own concerns about U.S. systems that Russia considers noncompliant.[31] Efforts to resolve compliance issues, including through the Special Verification Commission—the body established by the treaty to address these matters—were unsuccessful.

In 2017, the Trump administration sanctioned Russian entities involved in the allegedly noncompliant GLCM's development, production, and deployment and announced research and development on a conventional treaty-prohibited GLCM of its own.[32] In October 2018, the White House decided to "terminate" the treaty, identifying Russia's violation, as well as China's development of INF systems, as rationales.[33] According to U.S. Director of National Intelligence Daniel Coats, Russia's flight test program violated the treaty and seemed designed to conceal the missile's capabilities.[34] On December 4, 2018, Secretary of State Pompeo described Russia as in "material breach" of the INF Treaty and said the United States would suspend its obligations under the treaty after 60 days if Russia did not return to compliance in that time frame.[35] At the end of this waiting period, Pompeo announced that the United States would initiate the treaty's six-month withdrawal period beginning February 2, 2019. When this period ends, the treaty will be terminated.[36]

Moscow condemned the decision, labeling U.S. claims of noncompliance "fabrications" and warning of an impending arms race. The Kremlin then announced that Russia would suspend its own participation in the treaty and begin research and development of ground-based launchers for hypersonic intermediate and short-range missiles, calling this response "symmetrical" to U.S. plans.[37]

By deciding to withdraw first, the Trump administration took the Kremlin's bait. The decision redirects the blame for the treaty's demise to the United States, when instead it should be Russia's. Now Russia will be able to continue its violation and even build new INF missiles that would otherwise violate the treaty. An expansion of these weapons raises the risk of a destabilizing arms race in Europe and even Asia. Furthermore, the decision could serve Russian geopolitical interests by sharpening divisions between the United States and its European allies.

The White House may also have sacrificed an opportunity to leverage Russia's violation into a broader deal for renegotiating the INF Treaty and perhaps extending New START.

Policy Recommendations

In the wake of the U.S. decision to withdraw from the INF Treaty, policymakers should work to safeguard alliance relationships, reduce the risk of an arms race with Russia, and avoid jeopardizing an extension of the New START treaty. Although the Russian deployment is only a political threat to the United States, it is a security threat to NATO allies in Europe that will be further exacerbated by the breakdown of the INF Treaty. That is especially true if the U.S. decision sets off an arms race of INF-banned missiles, in which Russia would already have the lead.[38]

Going forward, the United States should take steps that protect both the security and the unity of the NATO alliance—no easy task. That objective requires U.S. action that pressures Moscow and draws support from NATO allies. Indeed, the United States cannot afford additional damage to its relationship with NATO following the U.S. withdrawal from the JCPOA and other recent incidents. In this case, it was prudent for U.S. officials to consult with European allies before the U.S. announcement to withdraw from the INF Treaty. On December 4, 2018, the NATO foreign ministers declared their support for the U.S. decision and called on Russia to return to compliance.[39]

Now that the treaty's withdrawal period has begun, Washington must work closely with NATO to prevent a renewed European arms race that could be stoked by Russia deploying INF-range weapons along NATO's eastern border. A potential expansion of Russian INF systems would hold European, not American, targets at risk. Therefore, any U.S. response should garner the unanimous support of NATO allies in Europe.

To reduce the risk of an arms race, the United States should be careful in its pursuit of a road-mobile GLCM, a system proposed by the Trump administration that would violate the INF Treaty. The 2018 National Defense Authorization Act called for a program of record to develop this type of system.[40] While some research and development activities are permitted by the INF Treaty, withdrawing from it would allow the United States to move into the flight testing and deployment stages. Although Russia and China are able to deploy these systems on their own territory, the United States would have to deploy its missiles on ally territory. It is unlikely that any NATO state, save perhaps Poland, would agree to this arrangement. Even in Poland, these systems would be so close to Russia that they would carry a high risk of inciting an arms race.[41] In fact, the Kremlin has confirmed that it would ramp up development of INF missiles if the United States were to show signs of doing the same. Provoking Moscow in this way could have the unintended effect of jeopardizing cooperation to extend New START.

Instead, the United States should respond to Russia's violation using systems that would not violate the INF Treaty but that would meet the same mission requirements. Specifically, the United States could expand its force of conventionally armed sea-launched cruise missiles and deploy Joint Air-to-Surface Standoff Missiles to counter Russia's INF deployment. Although these weapons have an intermediate range, they are compliant with the INF Treaty because they are deployed on ships and aircraft. This action would be acceptable to allies and consistent with the U.S. deployment of these weapons in Asia, which are aimed at countering Chinese land-based missile forces.[42]

Because the Trump administration does not have an effective plan to stop Russia from building up and fielding INF-range systems in the absence of the treaty, U.S. legislators and arms control experts should not abandon efforts to persuade the White House to find a solution with Moscow. Lawmakers should exercise their ability to restrict procurement for any administration plan that would provoke Russia and trouble our NATO allies, such as testing or deploying missiles that would violate the treaty.

Washington should leave the door open for negotiations on the rare chance that Russia shows a willingness to engage diplomatically. In fact, history illustrates that negotiations are still possible. In the 1980s, the United States accused Russia of violating the Anti-Ballistic Missile Treaty. But instead of withdrawing, Washington worked out compliance concerns with Moscow to make the treaty viable.[43] It is true that neither the current administration nor Russian skeptics on Capitol Hill have much appetite for this type of dialogue. Yet refusing to pursue a solution—or worse, provoking Russia with our own development of INF missiles—would be myopic given that New START hangs in the balance. As the extension deadline for that treaty draws near, it would be prudent for lawmakers and the White House to consider the possibility of cutting a larger arms control deal with Moscow that included both a path forward for the INF Treaty and an extension to New START. If Putin and Trump could agree on the importance of saving the INF Treaty, they could initiate a process to make the treaty viable once again through technical exchanges and systems inspections.[44]

As with the JCPOA, a unilateral decision to exit the INF Treaty damages America's reputation as an arms control leader and is sure to weaken future arms control and nonproliferation efforts involving Washington. In general, the decision signifies a trend away from arms control as a central tool of security and stability. Other key treaties, such as the Treaty on Open Skies that allows participants to conduct observation flights over the territories of signatories, could be the next casualties of this trend. To preserve the historic U.S. position as a leader in arms control, it is essential for U.S. policymakers to extend New START, which expires in February 2021.

The New Strategic Arms Reduction Treaty

U.S. nuclear policy experts and government officials should prioritize efforts to extend New START beyond its current expiration date in February 2021. An extension would help maintain some level of nuclear cooperation between the United States and Russia even as the countries' broader relationship continues to fray. In addition to contributing broadly to global stability, a New START extension would yield significant domestic benefits: namely, strengthening national security while limiting nuclear weapons spending.

New START entered into force in 2011 and requires both the United States and Russia to reduce their strategic nuclear arsenals to no more than 1,550 deployed warheads, 700 deployed delivery systems (nuclear-armed intercontinental ballistic missiles, submarine-launched ballistic missiles, and nuclear-capable bombers), and 800 deployed and nondeployed delivery systems.[45] As of February 2018, both states met these limits.[46] The treaty contains broad verification and transparency measures, including data exchanges every six months and up to 18 inspections per year per side. The exchanges have facilitated more than 16,000 notifications related to the location, movement, and disposition of nuclear weapons; and more than 275 onsite inspections have occurred since 2011.[47] While both the United States and Russia are modernizing their nuclear arsenals, both countries' strategic modernization plans are consistent with New START's restrictions. By restricting warhead counts and enabling a high degree of transparency, New START provides an essential contribution to U.S.–Russia nuclear stability.

New START will expire in February 2021 unless Moscow and Washington agree to extend it. Unfortunately, extension talks have stalled because of increasing tensions in the bilateral relationship. Furthermore, the Trump administration is resistant to extension. In a phone call with Putin in January 2017, President Trump rebuffed Putin's offer to discuss New START's extension.[48] Now, more than two years after that call, bilateral strategic stability talks, where New START would be a main topic, have repeatedly floundered. Discussions between U.S. National Security Advisor John Bolton and his Russian counterpart occurred only recently and do not appear promising.[49] In a speech to the Conservative Political Action Conference in 2017—a year before his appointment as national security advisor—Bolton called for the United States to, "abrogate the New START treaty so that we have a nuclear deterrent that's equal to our needs to prevent future conflict."[50] The implication is false: many experts and top military officials have repeatedly stated that New START is important for maintaining the U.S. deterrent.[51]

If New START disappears in 2021, there will be no limits on Russia's strategic nuclear forces. Washington will also lose critical monitoring and verification measures that allow the United States to keep an eye on the size and composition of Russia's nuclear stockpile. Meanwhile, top U.S. military personnel have repeatedly emphasized that this information is crucial to U.S. planning and resourcing.[52] Losing New START could trigger a costly nuclear arms buildup by both countries that would be difficult to monitor, stoking worst-case assumptions that feed into a vicious cycle of nuclear expansion. Deterrence is easier—and cheaper—to achieve with the limits and transparency measures put in place by New START.

Policy Recommendations

Washington has three basic options for approaching New START: allow the agreement to lapse without replacement; extend it; or replace it with another treaty. Bolton has suggested replacing New START with a treaty similar to the George W. Bush–era Moscow Treaty. However, that agreement lacked monitoring or verification measures, both essential aspects of New START.[53] Extending New START would preserve the agreement's transparency measures and prevent it from expiring before the two countries could complete a replacement treaty. An additional five years would give both sides time to negotiate a successive agreement and address Russian concerns that New START does not cover missile defense, conventional prompt global strike capabilities, or third-country forces.

Congressional resistance to New START also endangers its extension. The House version of the 2018 National Defense Authorization Act would have restricted funding for extending the agreement unless Russia returned to INF Treaty compliance.[54] Such a proposal, which was later dropped from the bill, would be counterproductive and endanger a successful treaty (New START) by linking it to a dying treaty (the INF Treaty).[55] The initiative signaled the skepticism of some lawmakers to New START. Yet at the same time, Congress possesses the most potent tool for pressuring the White House to secure an extension. For example, Congress could withhold funding for other Trump administration nuclear modernization and expansion plans, such as a new intercontinental ballistic missile program, unless the administration embarks on an effort to extend New START.

Such congressional resistance is one barrier that may frustrate efforts to extend the treaty. Another is emerging compliance concerns

surrounding New START. Although the State Department has certi-
fied Russia's compliance, the Russian Foreign Ministry has questioned
whether U.S. alterations to submarines and bombers affect U.S. compliance with the treaty. These concerns should be addressed diplomatically,
including through the Bilateral Consultative Commission, to enable an
extension of New START before the deadline.[56]

In the current political climate, U.S. officials and experts will need
to prove the value of New START by highlighting its limits on and insight into Russia's strategic forces. This transparency has enabled the
United States to avoid a costly arms buildup and strengthened its overall security vis-à-vis Russia. Policymakers should push back against efforts to link New START extension to Russian compliance with the INF
Treaty or other treaties. Arms control advocates should highlight New
START's success in slowing a costly nuclear buildup and emphasize
that extending the treaty is the least expensive and most straightfor-
ward option for maintaining strategic stability.

Conclusion

This chapter examined the strength of the JCPOA, the INF Treaty, and
New START amid dwindling support for arms control in Washington,
deteriorating U.S.–Russia relations, and growing global security challenges. Recent Trump administration decisions relating to each of these
agreements threaten to antagonize U.S. allies and undermine the legacy
of the United States as a global leader on arms control and nonproliferation. Without these agreements, there is a greater chance that states will
expand their nuclear arsenals. That result, if it occurs, would contribute
to greater global instability and incite the United States to increase its
own defense spending.

To advance national security, reduce costs, and protect the U.S. legacy
of arms control leadership, Washington should secure an extension of
the New START treaty as quickly as possible and work to maintain the
JCPOA's effects in some form until political circumstances allow for re-
affirmation of that agreement. In an environment of uncertainty around
the INF Treaty, the United States should pursue measures that maintain
pressure on Moscow and refrain from creating friction with NATO allies.

The primary challenge for policymakers will be managing fallout from the Trump administration's decisions by reassuring allies and finding space for compromise. Ultimately, the prospects for extending New START are more promising than those for repairing the JCPOA or the INF Treaty. Policymakers should focus their efforts on securing an extension of New START by stepping up efforts to pressure the Trump administration to prioritize these negotiations with Russia.

9. The Impact of the Nuclear Weapons Ban Movement on Arms Control and Nonproliferation

Beatrice Fihn

Despite legally binding agreements to prohibit biological and chemical weapons, until recently no similar disarmament treaty existed for the third, and most devastating, weapon of mass destruction.[1] However, on July 7, 2017, 122 states adopted the United Nations (UN) Treaty on the Prohibition of Nuclear Weapons (TPNW).[2] This marked the first time a global treaty has outlawed the possession and use of nuclear weapons.

Once the TPNW enters into force (likely to be in 2019 or 2020), the first 50 parties will be pushing hard to persuade states covered by a nuclear umbrella and the nuclear-armed states to renounce nuclear deterrence and come on board. No one—whether state or nonstate—is under any illusions about the challenges that lie ahead in achieving this breakthrough, but equally no one is blind to the urgency of the need, with the world standing on the verge of a new nuclear arms race.

This chapter summarizes how the world came to this precarious position. It describes the origins and progress of the movement to restrict and ultimately ban nuclear weapons and the huge challenges that remain in achieving a world without these weapons of mass destruction, especially given the current geopolitical climate.

History of the Movement

The movement to ban nuclear weapons began very soon after their use in the last few days of the Second World War. People everywhere looked on in horror at the devastation wrought on Hiroshima and Nagasaki on August 6 and 9, 1945, respectively: tens of thousands were incinerated instantly and tens of thousands more succumbed to burns or radiation poisoning in the days, months, and years that followed. The bombing of civilian areas was not unusual, but the use of nuclear weapons was a qualitative leap in mankind's ability to kill on a massive scale.

In January 1946, the first General Assembly resolution adopted by the newly created United Nations established the Atomic Energy Commission (UNAEC) with a mandate to tackle the problems raised by the discovery of atomic energy.[3] UNAEC was specifically charged with elaborating proposals to eliminate nuclear weapons from national arsenals.[4] In June 1946, at UNAEC's first session, the U.S. representative, Bernard Baruch, presented the so-called Baruch Plan. The plan proposed that the United States destroy all its nuclear weapons and that UN controls be imposed on the exploitation of atomic energy for other than peaceful purposes. Crucially, those controls would not be subject to a Security Council veto. The proposal made it clear, though, that the United States would maintain its nuclear weapons monopoly until the plan had been fully implemented. The Soviet Union rejected the Baruch Plan and countered with a proposal to ban all nuclear weapons. The United States itself rejected the Soviet proposal. In 1949, the Soviet Union tested its first nuclear device, and the UN General Assembly officially dissolved UNAEC in January 1952.[5] Comprehensive nuclear disarmament would not occur in the short or medium term.

A year later, in 1953, President Dwight D. Eisenhower delivered his famous "Atoms for Peace" speech to the UN General Assembly, proposing the creation of an international agency for atomic energy under UN auspices.[6] This new agency would be responsible for storing and protecting stockpiles of uranium and other fissionable material as well as for finding ways to apply atomic energy to agriculture, medicine, the generation of electricity, and other peaceful activities.[7] Since its establishment in 1957, the International Atomic Energy Agency (IAEA) has made a major contribution to the peaceful use of nuclear energy even though Eisenhower's broader vision of an international institution holding stockpiles of nuclear material remains, to date, unfulfilled.[8]

The Existing Nuclear Arms Control and Nonproliferation Regime

In parallel with the work of the IAEA, and amid the fear and paranoia of the Cold War, states made some progress on restricting the proliferation of nuclear weapons. The 1959 Antarctic Treaty—the first formal Cold War–era arms control agreement—decrees that "Antarctica shall be used for peaceful purposes only."[9] The treaty prohibits any nuclear explosions or the disposal of radioactive waste material across the area around the southern pole.[10] States also negotiated and adopted the Partial Test Ban Treaty following a proposal by India for an agreement to ban nuclear weapons tests. Agreement on verification procedures proved to be a major stumbling block. But after several years of difficult discussions, the treaty was finally adopted in 1963. Its successful adoption followed recognition of the huge toll atmospheric nuclear testing has on life, an impact that lingers for decades.[11] The Partial Test Ban Treaty obligates states parties (i.e., the countries that have ratified or acceded to the treaty and are therefore legally bound to its provisions) to prohibit, prevent, and abstain from nuclear weapons tests or any other nuclear explosions in the atmosphere, in outer space, and under water.[12]

In 1967, the Outer Space Treaty banned the stationing of nuclear weapons in space, on the moon, or on other celestial bodies, preventing, for a time, an arms race in space. Three years later, in 1970, the "cornerstone" of the current nuclear nonproliferation regime, the Treaty on the Non-Proliferation of Nuclear Weapons (NPT) entered into force.[13] A core aim of the NPT was to prevent horizontal proliferation of nuclear weapons, meaning that possession was limited to those states that already had them: China, France, the Soviet Union, the United Kingdom, and the United States. Thus, under Article I of the NPT, each nuclear-weapon state party (the five permanent members of the UN Security Council) undertakes not to transfer to any recipient nuclear weapons or other nuclear explosive devices; or to transfer control over such weapons or devices directly or indirectly; or to assist, encourage, or induce any nonnuclear-weapon state to manufacture or otherwise acquire such weapons or devices. In turn, in accordance with Article II,

97

state signatories without nuclear weapons undertake not to receive such weapons or other nuclear explosive devices or control over such weapons or devices directly, or indirectly; not to manufacture or otherwise acquire such weapons or devices; and not to seek or receive any assistance in their manufacture.

While imperfect, the NPT is justly credited with limiting the horizontal proliferation of nuclear weapons (four states beyond the five recognized by the NPT have since acquired and maintained a stockpile of nuclear weapons: India, Israel, North Korea, and Pakistan). However, the NPT did not stem the buildup of nuclear arsenals in the five recognized countries. At the height of the Cold War, the Soviet Union and the United States together possessed more than 60,000 nuclear weapons, which could extinguish all life on Earth several times over. The NPT does not impose any cap on stockpiles, much less specifically require the unilateral destruction of the existing arsenals by the five nuclear-weapon states. Article VI, though, does require each state party to "pursue negotiations in good faith on effective measures relating to cessation of the nuclear arms race at an early date and to nuclear disarmament."[14] It is the failure of the nuclear-weapon states named in the NPT to engage in good faith on nuclear disarmament that has been a principal source of frustration among nonnuclear-weapon states and ultimately led more than 120 states to adopt the TPNW treaty text on July 7, 2017.

In addition to the multilateral efforts discussed above, bilateral arms control agreements between the United States and Soviet Union led to major cuts in both countries' nuclear arsenals. For example, during President Richard Nixon's administration, and in the wake of the NPT, the Soviet Union and the United States began the process of controlling the nuclear arms race. In 1972 Nixon and Soviet leader Leonid Brezhnev signed both the Anti-Ballistic Missile Treaty and an interim agreement under the Strategic Arms Limitation Talks (SALT) process.[15] The latter froze each side's number of intercontinental ballistic missiles (ICBMs) and submarine-launched ballistic missiles (SLBMs) at the then-existing levels for five years, pending the negotiation of a second and more detailed Strategic Arms Limitation Treaty, SALT II.

The 1991 Strategic Arms Reduction Treaty (START I) further limited the United States and the Soviet Union to a maximum of 6,000 nuclear warheads on a total of 1,600 ICBMs, deployed SLBMs, and bombers for each country.[16] Most recently, New START (signed in 2010) brought the maximum number of deployed nuclear warheads for each state down to 1,550 by early February 2018.[17] Before that, the 1987 Intermediate-Range Nuclear Forces (INF) Treaty required the United States and the Soviet Union to eliminate all nuclear and conventional ground-launched ballistic and cruise missiles with ranges between 500 and 5,500 kilometers.[18] The INF Treaty was the first agreement between the two nuclear superpowers that sought to eliminate an entire category of nuclear weapons, backed by extensive on-site inspections to verify compliance.[19] However, in early February 2019 the United States and then the Russian Federation announced their withdrawal from the INF Treaty, which would allow both states to reintroduce these weapons from August 2, 2019, onward.

Over the past decade and a half, both multilateral and bilateral arms control regimes have slowed and, in some cases, are in retreat. New states have joined the nuclear club, and established nuclear-weapon states have expanded their arsenals. North Korea became a nuclear-weapon state, probably no later than 2006. The International Campaign to Abolish Nuclear Weapons (ICAN) was launched a year later, in 2007, and today has hundreds of partner organizations devoted to the elimination of nuclear weapons.[20] However, over the past two years in particular, nuclear arsenals in China, North Korea, and Pakistan have continued to grow, as have massive expenditures on nuclear weapons technology by Russia and the United States.

One example is multiple independently targetable reentry vehicles (MIRVs). START II, which was signed in 1993, prohibited the use of MIRVs on ICBMs, but the agreement never formally entered into force. Today, MIRV capability and integrated countermeasures, combined with the hypersonic speeds of ICBMs, are central to the ability of nuclear weapons to overwhelm missile defense systems. Meanwhile, battlefield nuclear weapons, which offer precious little military advantage but could all too easily spark a broader nuclear war, remain unprohibited. As Daniel Gerstein, a senior researcher at the RAND Corporation, noted in January 2018, both Russia and the United States may be expanding their tactical nuclear weapons capabilities.[21] Nuclear-weapon states, collectively, have dedicated trillions of dollars to the development and production of nuclear weapons and brought the world, once again, to the brink of a nuclear arms race.

The Treaty on the Prohibition of Nuclear Weapons

In December 2016, against this depressing backdrop, 113 states voted to convene a United Nations diplomatic conference "to negotiate a legally binding instrument to prohibit nuclear weapons, leading towards their total elimination."[22] In a message delivered on his behalf at the Peace Memorial Ceremony of Hiroshima on August 6, 2018, UN Secretary-General António Guterres said, "The adoption of the Treaty on the Prohibition of Nuclear Weapons last year demonstrated the international support that exists for a permanent end to the threat posed by nuclear arms, as well as frustration at the slow pace of achieving this goal."[23]

The TPNW is a comprehensive disarmament treaty, prohibiting all development, possession, transfer, and use of nuclear weapons, and requiring the verified destruction of any stockpiles. The treaty's first meeting of states parties is to be held within a year of the treaty's entry into force, and at that time deadlines will be set for destruction or removal of foreign weapons from a state party's territory. The treaty has no caveats or loopholes, such as those in the NPT, which would allow states parties to continue to support nuclear-weapon states with "source or special fissionable material."[24] We have—at last—a comprehensive global framework for the elimination of nuclear weapons.

The nuclear-weapon states stayed away from the TPNW negotiations, as did most states protected by nuclear umbrellas. They had no alternative to offer. In 1996 the UN General Assembly adopted the Comprehensive Test Ban Treaty (CTBT) following deadlock in the Conference on Disarmament, with India unwilling to join a consensus unless the nuclear-weapon states were prepared to begin negotiations on comprehensive nuclear disarmament. More than 20 years later, the CTBT is still not in force. And now the United States is making disquieting noises about restarting explosive nuclear testing.[25] Doing so would break a 26-year taboo and, presumably, embolden other states to do the same. Meanwhile, the Conference on Disarmament, which successfully negotiated the 1992 Chemical Weapons Convention, has been effectively deadlocked since 1996, unable to agree on even a negotiating agenda, much less a treaty. The United States, already more than $20 trillion in debt, is planning to spend more than $1 trillion over 30 years to modernize its nuclear arsenal.[26] Russia, despite reeling under the weight of international sanctions, feels compelled to follow suit.

So where do we go from here? No one expects nuclear weapons to be eradicated in one fell swoop. There are too many weapons in existence and too much fear and mistrust for that to happen. At the least, nuclear-armed states should accept that not a single additional nuclear weapon should be produced from this day forward. And the TPNW can create a powerful norm against nuclear weapons that increases incentives and creates pressure on nuclear-armed states to disarm. With the negotiation and adoption of a fissile material cutoff treaty, Eisenhower's vision of global stocks of plutonium and enriched uranium being placed under full IAEA oversight and supervision could finally be realized. A phased, step-by-step approach to meeting the obligations of the TPNW would be a logical approach for nuclear-weapon states. Bilateral treaties between the United States and Russia, between India and Pakistan, between China and India, and between North Korea and the United States, with phased destruction of nuclear weapons, could buttress these broader international processes.

Some people believe that nuclear weapons will never disappear. This same mentality slowed the adoption of the Biological Weapons Convention and the Chemical Weapons Convention. A lack of vision contributed to the time it took the world—93 years—after first agreeing to prohibit the use of chemical weapons as a means of warfare (in 1899) to agree to their verified destruction. It took us 46 years to achieve a similar result for biological weapons (1925 to 1971). The TPNW will contribute to stigmatizing and delegitimizing nuclear weapons in a way that the existing international legal regime does not. The NPT has been used by the nuclear-weapon states to retain their arsenals forever (conveniently forgetting the obligations of Article VI). Today, no global treaty other than the TPNW offers a comprehensive framework within which a nuclear-armed state can disarm. The TPNW will set the international community, finally, on the road to the elimination of these inhumane weapons of mass destruction. And it will not take us generations to reach that goal.

Notes

Foreword

1   Susan J. Koch, *The Presidential Nuclear Initiatives of 1991–1992*, Case Study Series 5 (Washington: Center for the Study of Weapons of Mass Destruction, 2012), https://ndupress.ndu.edu/Portals/68/Documents/casestudies/CSWMD_CaseStudy-5.pdf.

2   Frank Klotz, "Extending New START Is in America's National Security Interest," *Arms Control Today* (January-February 2019), https://www.armscontrol.org/act/2019-01/features/extending-new-start-americas-national-security-interest.

3   Dina Smeltz et al., *What Americans Think about America First: Results of the 2017 Chicago Council Survey of American Public Opinion and U.S. Foreign Policy* (Chicago: Chicago Council on Global Affairs, 2017), http://www.thechicagocouncil.org/sites/default/files/ccgasurvey2017_what_americans_think_about_america_first.pdf.

4   Frank Newport, "Americans Not Convinced U.S. Needs to Spend More on Defense," Gallup, February 21, 2018, https://news.gallup.com/poll/228137/americans-not-convinced-needs-spend-defense.aspx.

Introduction

1   John Hyten, "Nuclear Posture Review Discussion at National Defense University" (speech, National Defense University, Washington, DC, February 16, 2018), U.S. Strategic Command, https://www.stratcom.mil/Media/Speeches/Article/1446542/nuclear-posture-review-discussion-at-national-defense-university/. Emphasis added.

Chapter 1

1   According to warhead counting rules in New START, a nuclear bomber is counted once regardless of how many nuclear weapons it can carry. Office of the Secretary of Defense, *Nuclear Posture Review 2018*

(Washington: U.S. Department of Defense, February 2018), pp. 48–51, https://media.defense.gov/2018/Feb/02/2001872886/-1/-1/1/2018-NUCLEAR-POSTURE-REVIEW-FINAL-REPORT.PDF.

2   Michael Bennett, *Projected Costs of U.S. Nuclear Forces, 2017 to 2026* (Washington: Congressional Budget Office, February 2017), p. 2, https://www.cbo.gov/sites/default/files/115th-congress-2017-2018/reports/52401-nuclearcosts.pdf; and Office of the Secretary of Defense, *Nuclear Posture Review 2018*, pp. 51–52.

3   Michael Bennett, *Approaches for Managing the Costs of U.S. Nuclear Forces, 2017 to 2046* (Washington: Congressional Budget Office, October 2017), p. 1, https://www.cbo.gov/system/files/115th-congress-2017-2018/reports/53211-nuclearforces.pdf.

4   Bennett, *Projected Costs of U.S. Nuclear Forces, 2017 to 2026*; and Josh Rogin, "Obama Plans Major Nuclear Policy Changes in His Final Months," *Washington Post*, July 10, 2016, https://www.washingtonpost.com/opinions/global-opinions/obama-plans-major-nuclear-policy-changes-in-his-final-months/2016/07/10/fef3d5ca-4521-11e6-88d0-6adee48be8bc_story.html?utm_term=.87be644566e4.

5   Office of the Secretary of Defense, *Nuclear Posture Review 2018*.

6   Quoted in Bennett, *Approaches for Managing Costs*, p. 7.

7   Bennett, *Approaches for Managing Costs*, p. 9; and Office of the Secretary of Defense, *Nuclear Posture Review 2018*, p. 49.

8   Kingston Reif, "U.S. Nuclear Modernization Programs," Arms Control Association, August 2018, https://www.armscontrol.org/factsheets/USNuclearModernization.

9   Bennett, *Approaches for Managing Costs*, pp. 8–9.

10 Office of the Secretary of Defense, *Nuclear Posture Review 2018*, pp. 40–44.

11 Office of the Secretary of Defense, *Nuclear Posture Review 2018*, pp. 44–45.

12 Office of the Secretary of Defense, *Nuclear Posture Review 2018*, pp. 45–46.

13 Bennett, *Approaches for Managing Costs*, p. 26; and Office of the Secretary of Defense, *Nuclear Posture Review 2018*, pp. 46–47.

14 Bennett, *Approaches for Managing Costs*, p. 8.

15 Bennett, *Approaches for Managing Costs*, p. 4.

16 Office of the Secretary of Defense, *Nuclear Posture Review 2018*, p. 46.

17 Benjamin H. Friedman, "The China Hype," *Defense One*, September 4, 2018, https://www.defenseone.com/ideas/2018/09/china-hype/150996/; and Hans M. Kristensen and Robert S. Norris, "Chinese Nuclear Forces, 2018," *Bulletin of the Atomic Scientists* 74, no. 4 (2018): 289–95.

18 International Institute for Strategic Studies, *The Military Balance 2018* (Oxford, UK: Routledge, 2018), pp. 274–77, 333–37.

19 Quoted in Amy F. Woolf, *U.S. Strategic Nuclear Forces: Background, Developments and Issues*, CRS Report RL33640 (Washington: Congressional Research Service, November 21, 2018), p. 49, https://fas.org/sgp/crs/nuke/RL33640.pdf.

20 Bennett, *Approaches for Managing Costs*, p. 43.

21 Reif, "U.S. Nuclear Modernization Programs."

22 Adam Smith and Christopher Preble, "Another BRAC Now," *Strategic Studies Quarterly* 12, no. 1 (Spring 2018): 1–11, https://object.cato.org/sites/cato.org/files/articles/smith.pdf.

23 Bennett, *Approaches for Managing Costs*, p. 43.

24 Bennett, *Approaches for Managing Costs*, p. 43.

25 Bennett, *Approaches for Managing Costs*, p. 41.

26 Bennett, *Approaches for Managing Costs*, pp. 4–5.

27 Bennett, *Approaches for Managing Costs*, p. 41.

28 Bennett, *Approaches for Managing Costs*, p. 41.

29 Bennett, *Approaches for Managing Costs*, p. 8; and Oriana Pawlyk, "With Nuclear Mission in Rear-View, Options Abound for B-1B," Military.com, February 4, 2018, https://www.military.com/daily-news/2018/02/04/nuclear-mission-rear-view-options-abound-b-1-bomber.html.

30 International Institute for Strategic Studies, *The Military Balance 2018*.

31 Northrop Grumman, "The B-21 Raider: A Bomber for the Future," media kit. Accessed January 29, 2019, http://www.northropgrumman.com/MediaResources/MediaKits/B21/default.aspx?utm_source=PrintAd&utm_medium=Redirect&utm_campaign=B21_Redirect.

32 Jacob Cohn, Ryan Boone, and Amber Oar, *FY 2018 Weapon Systems Factbook* (Washington: Center for Strategic and Budgetary

Assessments, October 27, 2017), pp. 20–21, https://csbaonline.org/research/publications/fy-2018-weapon-systems-factbook.

33 Cohn, Boone, and Oar, *FY 2018 Weapon Systems Factbook.*

34 Jeremiah Gertler, *F-35 Joint Strike Fighter (JSF) Program*, CRS Report RL30563 (Washington: Congressional Research Service, April 23, 2018), p. 19, https://fas.org/sgp/crs/weapons/RL30563.pdf.

35 Office of the Secretary of Defense, *Nuclear Posture Review 2018*, p. 50.

36 Bennett, *Approaches for Managing Costs*, pp. 37–38.

37 Bennett, *Approaches for Managing Costs*, p. 38.

38 Bennett, *Approaches for Managing Costs*, p. 37.

39 Bennett, *Approaches for Managing Costs*, p. 30.

40 Bennett, *Approaches for Managing Costs*, p. 31.

41 Loren Thompson, "The Air Force's B-3 Bomber Isn't As Secret As It Seems," *Forbes*, March 9, 2015, https://www.forbes.com/sites/lorenthompson/2015/03/09/the-air-forces-b-3-bomber-isnt-as-secret-as-it-seems/.

42 Cohn, Boone, and Oar, *FY 2018 Weapon Systems Factbook*, pp. 20–21.

43 Bennett, *Approaches for Managing Costs*, p. 18.

44 Woolf, *U.S. Strategic Nuclear Forces.*

45 Bennett, *Approaches for Managing Costs*, p. 43.

46 Ronald O'Rourke, *Navy Columbia (SSBN-826) Class Ballistic Missile Submarine Program: Background and Issues for Congress*, CRS Report R41129 (Washington: Congressional Research Service, October 23, 2018), https://fas.org/sgp/crs/weapons/R41129.pdf.

47 Cohn, Boone, and Oar, *FY 2018 Weapon Systems Factbook*, pp. 94–95.

48 Cohn, Boone, and Oar, *FY 2018 Weapon Systems Factbook*, pp. 94–95.

49 O'Rourke, *Navy Columbia (SSBN-826) Class Ballistic Missile Submarine Program.*

50 Government Accountability Office, *National Nuclear Security Administration: Action Needed to Address Affordability of Nuclear Modernization Programs* (Washington: Government Accountability Office, April 2017), https://www.gao.gov/assets/690/684310.pdf.

51 Bennett, *Approaches for Managing Costs*, p. 43.

52 Bennett, *Approaches for Managing Costs*, p. 43.

Chapter 2

[1] Missile Defense Agency, "Fact Sheet: The Ballistic Missile Defense System," 18-MDA-9475 (Fort Belvoir, VA: Missile Defense Agency, June 14, 2018), https://www.mda.mil/global/documents/pdf/bmds.pdf.

[2] Paul Sonne, "Pentagon Looks to Adjust Missile Defense Policy to Include Threats from Russia, China," *Washington Post*, March 2, 2018, https://www.washingtonpost.com/world/national-security/pentagon-looks-to-adjust-missile-defense-policy-to-include-threats-from-russia-china/2018/03/01/2358ae22-1be5-11e8-8a2c-1a6665f59e95_story.html?utm_term=.621e3e0f93fa.

[3] Mike Stone, "U.S. Missile Defense Agency Budget Boosted to $11.5 Billion," Reuters, March 22, 2018, https://www.reuters.com/article/us-usa-pentagon-missiledefense/u-s-missile-defense-agency-budget-boosted-to-11-5-billion-idUSKBN1GZ065.

[4] Office of the Secretary of Defense, *2019 Missile Defense Review* (Washington: Department of Defense, January 2019), pp. 39–59, https://www.defense.gov/Portals/1/Interactive/2018/11-2019-Missile-Defense-Review/The%202019%20MDR_Executive%20Summary.pdf. Also see Patrick Tucker, "Trump's New Missile Policy Relies Heavily on Largely Unproven Technologies," Defense One, January 17, 2019, https://www.defenseone.com/technology/2019/01/trumps-new-missile-policy-relies-heavily-largely-unproven-technologies/154277/.

[5] Eric Gomez, "The New Missile-Defense Policy Won't Make Us Safer," Defense One, January 18, 2019, https://www.defenseone.com/ideas/2019/01/new-missile-defense-policy-wont-maker-us-safer/154295/?oref=d-river.

[6] Janne E. Nolan, *Guardians of the Arsenal: The Politics of Nuclear Strategy* (New York: Basic Books, 1989), p. 10.

[7] David E. Hoffman, *The Dead Hand: The Untold Story of the Cold War Arms Race and Its Dangerous Legacy* (New York: Anchor Books, 2009), pp. 263–68; Austin Long, "Red Glare: The Origin and Implications of Russia's 'New' Nuclear Weapons," War on the Rocks, March 26, 2018,

https://warontherocks.com/2018/03/red-glare-the-origin-and
-implications-of-russias-new-nuclear-weapons/; and William J. Perry,
My Journey at the Nuclear Brink (Stanford, CA: Stanford University
Press, 2015), pp. 66–68.

[8] Fiona S. Cunningham and M. Taylor Fravel, "Assuring Assured Retaliation: China's Nuclear Posture and U.S.-China Strategic Stability,"
International Security 40, no. 2 (Fall 2015): 16–19; and Long, "Red Glare."

[9] Current U.S. missile defense capabilities can protect against ballistic
missiles but offer limited protection against cruise missiles. Improving
cruise missile defense is a major Missile Defense Agency priority. James
Acton, "U.S. National Missile Defense Policy," in *Regional Missile Defense from a Global Perspective*, ed. Catherine McArdle Kelleher and Peter
Dombrowski (Stanford, CA: Stanford University Press, 2015), p. 41.

[10] Paula Hancocks and Joshua Berlinger, "Missile Defense System
that China Opposes Arrives in South Korea," CNN, March 7, 2017,
https://www.cnn.com/2017/03/06/asia/thaad-arrival-south
-korea/index.html.

[11] Ronald O'Rourke, *Navy Aegis Ballistic Missile Defense (BMD) Program:
Background and Issues for Congress*, CRS Report RL 33745 (Washington:
Congressional Research Service, July 5, 2018), p. i, https://fas.org
/sgp/crs/weapons/RL33745.pdf.

[12] For example, after several missile strikes against Turkey during
the Syrian civil war, NATO quickly deployed Patriot interceptors
in Turkey to defend against future attacks. See Eric Schmitt and
Michael R. Gordon, "U.S. to Send 2 Missile Units to Turkey to Deter
Syrians," *New York Times*, December 13, 2012, https://www.nytimes
.com/2012/12/14/world/middleeast/us-to-send-patriot-missiles
-to-turkey-to-deter-syria.html.

[13] Missile Defense Agency, "Fact Sheet: Ballistic Missile Defense
Intercept Flight Test Record," 18-MDA-9879 (Fort Belvoir, VA:
Missile Defense Agency, December 2018), accessed January 25, 2019,
https://www.mda.mil/global/documents/pdf/testrecord.pdf. The
realism of missile defense testing is highly questionable, and these
results should not be viewed as an accurate predictor of how systems would perform in combat. See Laura Grego and David Wright,

Incremental Progress but No Realistic Capability: Analysis of the Ground-Based Midcourse Missile Defense Test FTG-15 (Cambridge, MA: Union of Concerned Scientists, 2018), pp. 4–7.

14 Max Fisher et al., "Did American Missile Defense Fail in Saudi Arabia?" *New York Times*, December 4, 2017, https://www.nytimes.com/interactive/2017/12/04/world/middleeast/saudi-missile-defense.html; and Tim Weiner, "Patriot Missile's Success a Myth, Israeli Aides Say," *New York Times*, November 21, 1993, https://www.nytimes.com/1993/11/21/world/patriot-missile-s-success-a-myth-israeli-aides-say.html.

15 Thomas Karako and Ian Williams, "Next Steps for Homeland Missile Defense," Defense News, April 5, 2017, https://www.defensenews.com/land/2017/04/05/next-steps-for-homeland-missile-defense-commentary/.

16 James Acton, "Escalation through Entanglement: How the Vulnerability of Command-and-Control Systems Raises the Risks of an Inadvertent Nuclear War," *International Security* 43, no. 1 (Summer 2018): 64; and Thomas Karako, Ian Williams, and Wes Rumbaugh, *Missile Defense 2020: Next Steps for Defending the Homeland* (Washington: Center for Strategic and International Studies, April 2017), pp. 52–56.

17 Charles L. Glaser and Steve Fetter, "Should the United States Reject MAD? Damage Limitation and U.S. Nuclear Strategy toward China," *International Security* 41, no. 1 (Summer 2016): 76; and Ankit Panda and Vipin Narang, "Deadly Overconfidence: Trump Thinks Missile Defenses Work against North Korea, and That Should Scare You," War on the Rocks, October 16, 2017, https://warontherocks.com/2017/10/deadly-overconfidence-trump-thinks-missile-defenses-work-against-north-korea-and-that-should-scare-you/.

18 On the expansion of GMD interceptors, see Jen Judson, "Boeing Wins $6.6B Deal to Support Missile Defense System, Build More Interceptors," Defense News, February 1, 2018, https://www.defensenews.com/land/2018/02/01/boeing-wins-66-billion-deal-to-support-missile-defense-system-build-more-interceptors/; and David Willman, "Trump Administration Moves to Boost Homeland Missile Defense System Despite Multiple Flaws," *Los Angeles Times*, December 24, 2017,

http://www.latimes.com/politics/la-na-pol-missile-defense-flaws
-20171222-story.html. On the new missile defense radars, see Missile
Defense Agency, *Fiscal Year (FY) 2019 Budget Estimates Overview* (Fort
Belvoir, VA: Missile Defense Agency, March 2018), pp. 6–7.

[19] Karako, Williams, and Rumbaugh, *Missile Defense 2020*, p. 83; and
Patrick Tucker, "Pentagon Accelerates Work on Multi-Warhead
Interceptor," Defense One, May 26, 2017, https://www.defenseone
.com/technology/2017/05/Pentagon-Accelerates-Work-on-Multi
-Warhead-Interceptor/138213/.

[20] Caroline Houck, "Left-of-Launch Missile Defense: 'You Don't Want to
Have Just One Solution to the Threat,'" Defense One, January 24, 2018,
https://www.defenseone.com/threats/2018/01/left-launch-missile
-defense-you-dont-want-have-just-one-solution-threat/145438/;
and Missile Defense Agency, *FY 2019 Budget Estimates Overview*, p. 11.

[21] For discussions of U.S. strike capabilities, see Keir A. Lieber and
Daryl G. Press, "The New Era of Counterforce: Technological Change
and the Future of Nuclear Deterrence," *International Security* 41, no. 4
(Spring 2017): 18–32; Michael Russell Rip and James M. Hasik, *The
Precision Revolution: GPS and the Future of Aerial Warfare* (Annapolis,
MD: Naval Institute Press, 2002); and Caitlin Talmadge, "Would
China Go Nuclear? Assessing the Risk of Chinese Nuclear Escalation
in a Conventional War with the United States," *International Security*
41, no. 4 (Spring 2017): 50–92.

[22] Glaser and Fetter, "Should the United States Reject MAD?" pp. 54–59.

[23] T. Negeen Pegahi, "Deterrence in Retreat: How the Cold War's Core
Principle Fell out of Fashion," War on the Rocks, December 7, 2017,
https://warontherocks.com/2017/12/deterrence-retreat-cold-wars
-core-principle-fell-fashion/.

[24] Cunningham and Fravel, "Assuring Assured Retaliation," p. 19.

[25] The United States tried to calm Chinese concerns over THAAD
deployment in South Korea via technical briefings, but China rejected
the talks. See Michael D. Swaine, "Chinese Views on South Korea's
Deployment of THAAD," *China Leadership Monitor* 52 (Winter 2017): 4,
https://carnegieendowment.org/files/CLM52MS.pdf. Also see Long,
"Red Glare."

26 During the Cold War, skeptics of expanding U.S. missile defenses argued that the Soviet Union would be able to easily counteract U.S. defenses by building up their own nuclear forces. See Perry, *My Journey at the Nuclear Brink*, pp. 66–68.

27 Cunningham and Fravel, "Assuring Assured Retaliation," p. 47; and Glaser and Fetter, "Should the United States Reject MAD?" pp. 92–97.

28 Thomas Shugart and Javier Gonzalez, *First Strike: China's Missile Threat to U.S. Bases in Asia* (Washington: Center for a New American Security, June 2017), https://www.cnas.org/publications/reports/first-strike-chinas-missile-threat-to-u-s-bases-to-asia.

29 Joshua Rovner, "Two Kinds of Catastrophe: Nuclear Escalation and Protracted War in Asia," *Journal of Strategic Studies* 40, no. 5 (2017): 7.

30 This is sometimes called the "use-or-lose" dilemma. See Talmadge, "Would China Go Nuclear?" pp. 53–55.

31 Karen Montague and Erika Solem, "Chinese Hypersonic Weapons Development," *China Brief* 16, no. 7 (April 21, 2016): 7–8.

32 Aaron Mehta, "3 Thoughts on Hypersonic Weapons from the Pentagon's Technology Chief," Defense News, July 16, 2018, https://www.defensenews.com/air/2018/07/16/3-thoughts-on-hypersonic-weapons-from-the-pentagons-technology-chief/.

33 Vladimir Putin, "Presidential Address to the Federal Assembly," (speech, Moscow, Russia, March 1, 2018), President of Russia, http://en.kremlin.ru/events/president/news/56957.

34 For more detailed discussions of Chinese threat perceptions of U.S. missile defense, see Cunningham and Fravel, "Assuring Assured Retaliation," pp. 16–19; and David Logan, "Hard Constraints on China's Nuclear Forces," War on the Rocks, November 8, 2017, https://warontherocks.com/2017/11/china-nuclear-weapons-breakout/. On Russian threat perceptions, see Eric Gomez, "Why Putin Is Obsessed with America's Missile Defense," *The National Interest*, March 3, 2018, https://nationalinterest.org/blog/the-buzz/why-putin-obsessed-americas-missile-defense-24737; and Long, "Red Glare."

35 Garrett M. Graff, "The New Arms Race Threatening to Explode in Space," *Wired*, June 26, 2018, https://www.wired.com/story/new-arms-race-threatening-to-explode-in-space/.

36 Acton, "Escalation through Entanglement," p. 58.

37 Tong Zhao and Li Bin, "The Underappreciated Risks of Entanglement: A Chinese Perspective," in *Entanglement: Russian and Chinese Perspectives on Non-Nuclear Weapons and Nuclear Risks*, ed. James M. Acton (Washington: Carnegie Endowment for International Peace, 2017), pp. 58–59.

38 Grego and Wright, *Incremental Progress but No Realistic Capability*, p. 7.

39 Acton, "Escalation through Entanglement," p. 64; and Zhao and Li, "The Underappreciated Risks of Entanglement," p. 51.

40 Missile Defense Agency, "Fact Sheet: Ballistic Missile Defense Intercept Flight Test Record."

41 For an overview of potential technologies that could improve the GMD and its associated sensors, see Karako, Williams, and Rumbaugh, *Missile Defense 2020*, pp. 104–20.

42 Laura Grego, "U.S. Ground-based Midcourse Missile Defense: Expensive and Unreliable," *Bulletin of the Atomic Scientists* 74, no. 4 (2018): 224–25.

43 Missile Defense Agency, *FY 2019 Budget Estimates Overview*, p. 4.

44 Acton, "Escalation through Entanglement," pp. 61–65.

45 For more on entanglement and nuclear escalation risks, see Acton, "Escalation through Entanglement."

46 Missile Defense Agency, "Fact Sheet: Ballistic Missile Defense Intercept Flight Test Record."

47 Saeed Al-Batiti and Rick Gladstone, "Saudis Claim to Intercept 7 Missiles Fired at Cities from Yemen," *New York Times*, March 25, 2018, https://www.nytimes.com/2018/03/25/world/middleeast/saudi-arabia-yemen-missile-houthi.html; Fisher et al., "Did American Missile Defense Fail in Saudi Arabia?"; and Yaakov Lappin, "IDF Satisfied with Iron Dome's Performance during Latest Escalation," *IHS Jane's Defence Weekly*, November 15, 2018, https://www.janes.com/article/84620/idf-satisfied-with-iron-dome-s-performance-during-latest-escalation.

48 Carl Rehberg and Mark Gunzinger, *Air and Missile Defense at a Crossroads: New Concepts and Technologies to Defend America's Overseas Bases* (Washington: Center for Strategic and Budgetary Assessments, 2018), https://csbaonline.org/research/publications/air-and-missile-defense-at-a-crossroads-new-concepts-and-technologies-to-de/publication.

Chapter 3

1   Todd Harrison et al., *Escalation and Deterrence in the Second Space Age* (Washington: Center for Strategic and International Studies, 2017), p. 2.

2   Robert Bowman, *Star Wars: A Defense Insider's Case against the Strategic Defense Initiative* (Los Angeles: Tarcher Publications, 1986), p. 14.

3   Preparatory Commission for the Comprehensive Nuclear-Test-Ban Treaty Organization, "Testing Times: 9 July 1962, 'Starfish Prime,' Outer Space," CTBTO, Vienna, Austria, 2017, https://www.ctbto.org/specials/testing-times/9-july-1962starfish-prime-outer-space.

4   Laura Grego, *A History of Anti-Satellite Programs* (Cambridge, MA: Union of Concerned Scientists, January 2012), pp. 3–4.

5   Harrison et al., *Escalation and Deterrence in the Second Space Age*, p. 2; and Ellen Pawlikowski, Doug Loverro, and Tom Cristler, "Space: Disruptive Challenges, New Opportunities, and New Strategies," *Strategic Studies Quarterly* 6, no. 1 (Spring 2012): 30.

6   Treaty Banning Nuclear Weapon Tests in the Atmosphere, in Outer Space and Under Water, U.S.-U.K.-U.S.S.R., August 5, 1963, 14 U.S.T. 1313.

7   Agreement on Measures to Reduce the Risk of Outbreak of Nuclear War between the United States of America and the Union of Soviet Socialist Republics (Accidents Measures Agreement), U.S.-U.S.S.R., September 30, 1971, 807 U.N.T.S. 57; Agreement between the United States of America and the Union of Soviet Socialist Republics on Measures to Improve the U.S.A.-U.S.S.R. Direct Communications Link, U.S.-U.S.S.R., September 30, 1971, 806 U.N.T.S. 402.

8   Grego, *A History of Anti-Satellite Programs*, p. 3.

9   Amrom Katz, "Preliminary Thoughts on Crises: More Questions Than Answers," (report, Secretary of the Air Force Office of Special Projects, March 1972), pp. 4–5, https://aerospace.csis.org/wp-content/uploads/2018/09/Amrom-Katz-NRO-Paper-on-Satellite-Defenses-1972.pdf.

10 The White House, "Fact Sheet on the Strategic Arms Reduction Treaty (START)," July 31, 1991, American Presidency Project, University of CaliforniaSantaBarbara,https://www.presidency.ucsb.edu/documents/white-house-fact-sheet-the-strategic-arms-reduction-treaty-start.

[11] George Bush, "Address to the Nation on Reducing United States and Soviet Nuclear Weapons," (speech, White House, Washington, September 27, 1991), https://www.presidency.ucsb.edu/documents /address-the-nation-reducing-united-states-and-soviet-nuclear -weapons.

[12] The term "second space age" is borrowed from Tom Cremins, *A New Space Age: Maximizing Global Benefits* (New York: World Economic Forum, 2014), http://reports.weforum.org/global-strategic-foresight /thomas-e-cremins-nasa-a-new-space-age/.

[13] Patrick Rayermann, "Exploiting Commercial SATCOM: A Better Way," *Parameters* 33 (Winter 2003–2004): 55.

[14] Katz, "Preliminary Thoughts on Crises."

[15] T. S. Kelso, "Analysis of the 2007 Chinese ASAT Test and the Impact of Its Debris on the Space Environment," Technical Paper, 2007 AMOS Conference (Colorado Springs, CO: Center for Space Standards & Innovation, 2007), https://celestrak.com/publications/AMOS/2007 /AMOS-2007.pdf.

[16] For more information on counterspace weapons and which nations have them, see Todd Harrison, Kaitlyn Johnson, and Thomas Roberts, *Space Threat Assessment 2018* (Washington: Center for Strategic and International Studies, April 2018), https://aerospace.csis.org /wp-content/uploads/2018/04/Harrison_SpaceThreatAssessment _FULL_WEB.pdf.

[17] Sydney J. Freedberg Jr., "U.S. Jammed Own Satellites 261 Times; What If Enemy Did?" Breaking Defense, December 2, 2015, https://breakingdefense.com/2015/12/us-jammed-own-satellites -261-times-in-2015-what-if-an-enemy-tried/.

[18] UN General Assembly, Resolution 2222 (XXI), Treaty on Principles Governing the Activities of States in the Exploration and Use of Outer Space, including the Moon and Other Celestial Bodies, A/RES/21/2222 (December 19, 1966), http://www.un-documents .net/a21r2222.htm.

[19] See David Wright, Laura Grego, and Lisbeth Gronlund, *The Physics of Space Security: A Reference Manual* (Cambridge, MA: American Academy of Arts and Sciences, 2005).

Chapter 4

1 Office of the Secretary of Defense, *Nuclear Posture Review 2018* (Washington: Department of Defense, February 2018), https://media .defense.gov/2018/Feb/02/2001872886/-1/-1/1/2018-NUCLEAR -POSTURE-REVIEW-FINAL-REPORT.PDF.

2 Vladimir Putin, "Presidential Address to the Federal Assembly" (speech, Moscow, Russia, March 1, 2018), President of Russia, http:// en.kremlin.ru/events/president/news/56957; Vladimir Putin, "Presidential Address to the Federal Assembly" (speech, Moscow, Russia, February 20, 2019), President of Russia, http://en.kremlin.ru/events /president/news/59863; and Mikhail Sosnovskii, Aleksandr Khazov, and Aleksandr Khriapin, "V usloviiakh narastaiushchei konfrontatsii," *Natsional'naia oborona*, no. 5 (May 2018): 48–53.

3 Alexey Arbatov, Vladimir Dvorkin, and Petr Topychkanov, "Entanglement as a New Security Threat: A Russian Perspective," in *Entanglement: Russian and Chinese Perspectives on Non-Nuclear Weapons and Nuclear Risks*, ed. James Acton (Washington: Carnegie Endowment for International Peace, 2017), pp. 11–27, https://carnegieendowment .org/2017/11/08/entanglement-chinese-and-russian-perspectives -on-non-nuclear-weapons-and-nuclear-risks-pub-73162.

4 Arbatov, Dvorkin, and Topychkanov, "Entanglement as a New Security Threat."

5 Aleksandr Bartosh, "Oskolki gibrida," *Voenno-promyshlennyi kur'er*, May 30, 2018, p. 4, https://dlib.eastview.com/browse/doc/51153274; Vladimir Kozin, "Strategiia sily," *Krasnaia Zvezda*, February 17, 2015, https://dlib.eastview.com/browse/doc/43126623; A. Marinin, "Natsional'naia voennaia strategiia SShA—2015," *Zarubezhnoe voennoe obozrenie* no.12 (December 2015): 3–10, https://dlib.eastview.com /browse/doc/45952791; Dmitrii Trenin, "Strategiia Obamy i interesy rossii," *Voenno-promyshlennyi kur'er*, June 16, 2010, p. 9, https://dlib .eastview.com/browse/doc/21997205; and Sosnovskii, Khazov, and Khriapin, "V usloviiakh narastaiushchei konfrontatsii."

6 Vladimir Shcherbakov, "Pobedit li Rossiia v novoi bitve za Atlantiku," *Nezavisimoe voennoe obozrenie*, May 18, 2018, https://dlib .eastview.com/browse/doc/51065086.

7 Arbatov, Dvorkin, and Topychkanov, "Entanglement as a New Security Threat"; Nina Tannenwald, "The Great Unraveling: The Future of the Nuclear Normative Order," in *Meeting the Challenges of the New Nuclear Age: Emerging Risks and Declining Norms in the Age of Technological Innovation and Changing Nuclear Doctrines*, ed. Nina Tannenwald and James M. Acton (Cambridge, MA: American Academy of Arts and Sciences, 2018); and Katarzyna Zysk, "Escalation and Nuclear Weapons in Russia's Military Strategy," *RUSI Journal* (May 2018), https://rusi.org/publication/rusi-journal/escalation-and-nuclear-weapons-russia%E2%80%99s-military-strategy?page=209.

8 Viacheslav Baskakov and Aleksandr Gorshkov, "Moskva ne sformulirovala novuiu strategiiu i iadernuiu kontseptsiiu," *Nezavisimoe voennoe obozrenie*, 2004, https://dlib.eastview.com/browse/doc/6099323; Igor Bocharov, "Pentagon moderniziruet iadernuiu strategiu," *Nezavisimoe voennoe obozrenie*, 2013, https://dlib.eastview.com/browse/doc/37696220; Markell Boitsov, "Tri kita Amerikansogo iadernogo ustrasheniia," *Nezavisimoe voennoe obozrenie*, 2015, https://dlib.eastview.com/browse/doc/44722019; Markell Boitsov, "Usloviia perekhoda k primeneniiu iadernogo oruzhiia Soedinennymi Shtatami Ameriki," *Morskoi sbornik*, 2014, https://dlib.eastview.com/browse/doc/42896513; German Ioilev, "Luchshe by ne bylo voiny," *Atomnaia strategiia*, 2015, https://dlib.eastview.com/browse/doc/49638219; L. N. Lysenko and V. A. Petrov, "Transformatsiia kontseptsii i postanovka zadach modernizatsii raketnykh kompleksov morskoi sostavliaiushchei iadernoi triady," *Izvestiia Rossiiskoi akademii raketnykh i artilleriiskikh nauk* no.1 (2018): 3–5, https://dlib.eastview.com/browse/doc/50730499; and Midykhat Vil'Danov and Vladimir Lumpov, "Mirotvorcheskie initsiativy Baraka Obamy i strategicheskoe iadernoe planirovanie," *Natsional'naia oborona*, 2010, https://dlib.eastview.com/browse/doc/27615590.

9 Tannenwald, "The Great Unraveling."

10 See Arbatov, Dvorkin, and Topychkanov, "Entanglement as a New Security Threat"; James T. Quinlivan and Olga Oliker, *Nuclear Deterrence in Europe: Russian Approaches to a New Environment and Implications for the United States* (Santa Monica, CA: RAND Corporation, 2011), pp. 20, 22–24; and Zysk, "Escalation and Nuclear Weapons."

11 Makhmut A. Gareev, "Itogi deiatel'nosti Akademii voennykh nauk za 2017 god i zadachi akademii na 2018 god," *Vestnik Akademii voennykh nauk* no. 2 (2018): 6–15, https://dlib.eastview.com/browse /doc/51523023; V. I. Lumpov and V. V. Karpov, "Sushchnost' amerikanskoi kontseptsii strategicheskogo sderzhivaniia," *Voennaia mysl'* no. 9 (September 2012): 65–72, https://dlib.eastview.com/browse /doc/27965221; and M. Vildanov and A. Kuznetsov, "Obzor iadernoi politiki SShA i osnovnye napravleniia stroitel'stva i razvitiia strategicheskikh nastupatel'nykh sil," *Zarubezhnoe voennoe obozrenie* no. 5 (May 2018): 3–11, https://dlib.eastview.com/browse/doc/51196477.

12 Elbridge Colby, "Countering Russian Nuclear Strategy in Central Europe," Center for a New American Security, November 11, 2015, https://www.cnas.org/publications/commentary/countering -russian-nuclear-strategy-in-central-europe; and Matthew Kroenig, "The Case for Tactical U.S. Nukes," *Wall Street Journal,* January 24, 2018, https://www.wsj.com/articles/the-case-for-tactical-u-s-nukes -1516836395.

13 Kroenig, "The Case for Tactical U.S. Nukes"; and Jüri Luik and Tomas Jermalavičius, "A Plausible Scenario of Nuclear War in Europe, and How to Deter It: A Perspective from Estonia," *Bulletin of the Atomic Scientists* 73, no. 4 (2017): 233–39.

14 Colby, "Countering Russian Nuclear Strategy in Central Europe"; Kroenig, "The Case for Tactical U.S. Nukes"; Office of the Secretary of Defense, *Nuclear Posture Review 2018*; and Zysk, "Escalation and Nuclear Weapons."

15 For an overview of perspectives on this theme, see James M. Acton, "Technology, Doctrine and the Risk of Nuclear War," in *Meeting the Challenges of the New Nuclear Age: Emerging Risks and Declining Norms in the Age of Technological Innovation and Changing Nuclear Doctrines,* ed. Nina Tannenwald and James M. Acton (Cambridge, MA: American Academy of Arts and Sciences, 2018), pp. 32–55; Olga Oliker, *Russia's Nuclear Doctrine: What We Know, What We Don't, and What That Means* (Washington: Center for Strategic and International Studies, May 2016), https://csis-prod.s3.amazonaws.com/s3fs-public/publication/160504 _Oliker_RussiasNuclearDoctrine_Web.pdf; Bruno Tertrais, "Russia's

117

Nuclear Policy: Worrying for the Wrong Reasons," *Survival* 60, no. 2 (2018): 33–44; and Zysk, "Escalation and Nuclear Weapons."

16 Colby, "Countering Russian Nuclear Strategy in Central Europe"; Kroenig, "The Case for Tactical U.S. Nukes"; and Luik and Jermalavičius, "A Plausible Scenario of Nuclear War in Europe."

17 Gareev, "Itogi deiatel'nosti Akademii voennykh nauk."

18 Ioilev, "Luchshe by ne bylo voiny"; Aleksandr Khramchikhin, "Pochemu nam ne strashen 'bystryi global'nyi udar,'" *Nezavisimoe voennoe obozrenie*, 2017, https://dlib.eastview.com/browse/doc/49928026; and Igor Korotchenko, "Moskva prikryta ot udarov vozdushnogo protivnika s veroyatnost'u 99%," *Natsional'naia oborona*, April 2018, http://www.oborona.ru/includes/periodics/authors/2015/0423/132315591/detail.shtml.

19 "Genkonsturktor 'Almaz-Anteya': Rossiya sledit za perevooruzheniem armii SShA," *RIA Novosti*, April 24, 2017, https://ria.ru/defense_safety/20170424/1492950660.html; V. V. Barvinenko, "O popytkakh revizii polozhenii teorii vozdushno-kosmicheskoi oborony," *Voennaia mysl'* no. 4 (April 2018): 84–90, https://dlib.eastview.com/browse/doc/51074551; Sergei Iagol'nikov, "Protivoudarnye eshelony," *Voenno-promyshlennyi kur'er*, June 8, 2016, https://dlib.eastview.com/browse/doc/46735174; and Konstantin Sivkov, "Chernye dyry i krasnye linii," *Voenno-promyshlennyi kur'er*, May 3, 2017, https://dlib.eastview.com/browse/doc/48699522.

20 Putin, "Presidential Address to the Federal Assembly" (speech, Moscow, Russia, March 1, 2018).

21 Missile defenses were limited under the Anti-Ballistic Missile Treaty, from which the United States unilaterally withdrew in 2002.

22 Office of the Secretary of Defense, *Nuclear Posture Review 2018*, pp. xii–xiii.

23 Valerie Insinna, "To Deter Russia, US Needs New Low-yield Nukes, Says STRATCOM Head," Defense News, March 20, 2018, https://www.defensenews.com/smr/nuclear-arsenal/2018/03/20/stratcom-head-to-deter-russia-us-needs-new-low-yield-nukes; and Kroenig, "The Case for Tactical U.S. Nukes."

24 Bruce Blair, "How Obama Could Revolutionize Nuclear Weapons Strategy before He Goes," *Politico Magazine*, June 22, 2016, https://www.politico.com/magazine/story/2016/06/barack-obama-nuclear-weapons-213981; and Office of the Secretary of Defense, *Nuclear Posture Review 2018.*

25 On whether or not coercion by nuclear weapon states is effective, see the competing arguments presented by Matthew Kroenig, *The Logic of American Nuclear Strategy: Why Strategic Superiority Matters* (Oxford: Oxford University Press, 2018); and Todd S. Sechser and Matthew Fuhrmann, *Nuclear Weapons and Coercive Diplomacy* (Cambridge: Cambridge University Press, 2017). Regardless of whether Sechser and Fuhrmann are right that nuclear weapons do not create coercive advantages or Kroenig is right that they do, the combined analysis suggests that leaders of nuclear weapon states, including the United States, believe in Kroenig's argument, at least some of the time. See also Tannenwald, "The Great Unraveling."

26 Ministry of Foreign Affairs of the Russian Federation, "Voennaya doktrina Rossiiskoi Federatsii," December 26, 2014, http://www.mid.ru/documents/10180/822714/41d527556bec8deb3530.pdf/d899528d-4f07-4145-b565-1f9ac290906c.

27 Russian strategic nuclear planning appears to emphasize launch-on-warning and launch-under-attack scenarios, with an emphasis on silo-based ICBMs. Ballistic missile submarines and mobile ICBMs would form the core of a retaliatory strike. Russian weapons, having few or no U.S. nuclear forces to strike, would likely target industrial and population centers. This approach is somewhat out of line with Russia's force posture, which, despite the increased deployment of survivable systems, continues to place large numbers of warheads on silo-based ICBMs. See V. F. Lata, "Nastoiashchee i budushchee RVSN kak garanta oboronnoi bezopasnosti Rossii," *Vestnik Akademii voennykh nauk*, 2018, https://dlib.eastview.com/browse/doc/51523032; Lysenko and Petrov, "Transformatsiia kontseptsii"; and Sivkov, "Chernye dyry i krasnye linii."

28 Vladimir Solovyov, "'Zachem nam takoy mir, esli tam ne budet Rossii?' Putin—o global'noy katastrofe posle yadernogo udara," *Meduza*, March 7, 2018, https://meduza.io/news/2018/03/07/zachem-nam -takoy-mir-esli-tam-ne-budet-rossii-putin-o-globalnoy-katastrofe -posle-yadernogo-udara.

29 Lysenko and Petrov, "Transformatsiia kontseptsii."

30 Oliker, *Russia's Nuclear Doctrine*.

31 Oliker, *Russia's Nuclear Doctrine*.

32 "Ukaz Prezidenta Rossiiskoy Federatsii ot 20.07.2017 g. No. 327," President of Russia, http://kremlin.ru/acts/bank/42117.

33 "Osnovy gosudarstvennoi politiki rossiiskoi federatsii v oblasti voenno-morskoi deyatel'nosti na period do 2020 goda,"*Flot—XXI Vek*, January 20, 2013, http://blackseafleet-21.com/news/20-01 -2013_osnovy-gosudarstvennoj-politiki-rossijskoj-federatsii-v-oblasti -voenno-morskoj-dejatelnos; and Zysk, "Escalation and Nuclear Weapons."

34 For informed discussions from various perspectives, see Oliker, *Russia's Nuclear Doctrine*; Olga Oliker and Andrey Baklitskiy, "The Nuclear Posture Review and Russian 'De-escalation': A Dangerous Solution to a Nonexistent Problem," War on the Rocks, February 20, 2018, https://waron therocks.com/2018/02/nuclear-posture-review-russian-de-escalation -dangerous-solution-nonexistent-problem/; Tertrais, "Russia's Nuclear Policy"; and Zysk, "Escalation and Nuclear Weapons."

35 Gregory Koblentz, "Putin's new doctrine (with apologies to Michelle Obama): 'When you go low yield, we go high yield,'" Twitter, March 6, 2018, 5:21 p.m., https://twitter.com/gregkoblentz/status /971194217006551040.

36 Aleksander Mozgovoi, "Oruzhie 'Proshchai' Amerika," *Natsional'naia Oborona*, no. 3, March 2018, http://www.oborona.ru/includes /periodics/navy/2018/0314/173723825/detail.shtml; and Solovyov, "Zachem nam takoy mir."

37 Acton, "Technology, Doctrine, and the Risk of Nuclear War"; Arbatov, Dvorkin, and Topychkanov, "Entanglement as a New Security Threat"; Pavel Podvig, "Blurring the Line between Nuclear and Nonnuclear Weapons: Increasing the Risk of Accidental Nuclear War?," *Bulletin*

of the Atomic Scientists 72, no. 3 (2016): 145–49; Tannenwald, "The Great Unraveling"; Jane Vaynman, "Introduction," in *Meeting the Challenges of the New Nuclear Age: Emerging Risks and Declining Norms in the Age of Technological Innovation and Changing Nuclear Doctrines,* ed. Nina Tannenwald and James M. Acton (Cambridge, MA: American Academy of Arts and Sciences, 2018), https://www.amacad.org /multimedia/pdfs/publications/researchpapersmonographs /New-Nuclear-Age_Emerging-Risks/New-Nuclear-Age_Emerging -Risks.pdf; Zysk, "Escalation and Nuclear Weapons"; and Katarzyna Zysk, "Nonstrategic Nuclear Weapons in Russia's Evolving Military Doctrine," *Bulletin of the Atomic Scientists* 73, no. 5 (2017): pp. 322–27, https://doi.org/10.1080/00963402.2017.1362908.

[38] Pavel Podvig and Javier Serrat, *Lock Them Up: Zero-Deployed Non-Strategic Nuclear Weapons in Europe* (Geneva: United Nations Institute for Disarmament Research, 2017), http://www.unidir.org/files /publications/pdfs/lock-them-up-zero-deployed-non-strategic -nuclear-weapons-in-europe-en-675.pdf.

Chapter 5

[1] Office of the Secretary of Defense, *Nuclear Posture Review 2018* (Washington: Department of Defense, February 2018), https:// media.defense.gov/2018/Feb/02/2001872886/-1/-1/1/2018 -NUCLEAR-POSTURE-REVIEW-FINAL-REPORT.PDF; and Office of the Secretary of Defense, *Summary of the 2018 National Defense Strategy of the United States of America: Sharpening the American Military's Competitive Edge* (Washington: Department of Defense, 2018), https:// dod.defense.gov/Portals/1/Documents/pubs/2018-National -Defense-Strategy-Summary.pdf.

[2] Charles L. Glaser and Steve Fetter, "Should the United States Reject MAD? Damage Limitation and U.S. Nuclear Strategy toward China," *International Security* 41, no. 1 (Summer 2016): 49–98.

[3] Hugh White, "To Reassure U.S. Allies in Asia, Admit Mutual Vulnerability with China," War on the Rocks, June 8, 2018, https:// warontherocks.com/2018/06/to-reassure-u-s-allies-in-asia-admit -mutual-vulnerability-with-china/.

4   Office of the Secretary of Defense, *Nuclear Posture Review 2018*, p. viii.

5   John R. Harvey, "Commentary: Negating North Korea's Nukes," Defense News, February 15, 2016, https://www.defensenews.com /opinion/commentary/2016/02/15/commentary-negating-north -koreas-nukes/; and Vince A. Manzo and John K. Warden, "The Least Bad Option: Damage Limitation and U.S. Deterrence Strategy toward North Korea," in "Policy Roundtable: Are There Any Good Choices When It Comes to North Korea?," *Texas National Security Review*, February 7, 2018, https://tnsr.org/roundtable/policy-roundtable -good-choices-comes-north-korea/#essay6.

6   For an overview, see Austin Long, *Deterrence from Cold War to Long War: Lessons from Six Decades of RAND Research* (Santa Monica, CA: RAND Corporation, 2008), https://www.rand.org/pubs/monographs /MG636.html.

7   Fiona S. Cunningham and M. Taylor Fravel, "Assuring Assured Retaliation: China's Nuclear Posture and U.S.-China Strategic Stability," *International Security* 40, no. 2 (Fall 2015): 12–15; and M. Taylor Fravel and Evan S. Medeiros, "China's Search for Assured Retaliation: The Evolution of Chinese Nuclear Strategy and Force Structure," *International Security* 35, no. 2 (Fall 2010): 48–87.

8   See Brad Roberts, *The Case for U.S. Nuclear Weapons in the 21st Century* (Stanford, CA: Stanford University Press, 2015), chapters 5 and 7.

9   Office of the Secretary of Defense, *Nuclear Posture Review 2018*, p. 23.

10 Caitlin Talmadge, "Would China Go Nuclear? Assessing the Risk of Chinese Nuclear Escalation in a Conventional War with the United States," *International Security* 41, no. 4 (Spring 2017): 50–92.

11 For an account of Chinese views on escalation risks, see Cunningham and Fravel, "Assuring Assured Retaliation," pp. 34–45.

12 Elbridge A. Colby and Michael S. Gerson, eds., *Strategic Stability: Contending Interpretations* (Carlisle, PA: U.S. Army War College Press, 2013).

13 For early articulations of the concept, see Thomas Schelling, *The Strategy of Conflict* (New York: Oxford University Press, 1960); and Albert Wohlstetter, "The Delicate Balance of Terror," *Foreign Affairs* 37, no. 2 (January 1959), https://www.foreignaffairs.com/articles /1959-01-01/delicate-balance-terror.

[14] For a contemporary discussion of strategic stability, see Brad Roberts, "Strategic Stability under Obama and Trump," *Survival* 59, no. 4 (August/September 2017): 47–74; and Heather Williams, "Strategic Stability, Uncertainty and the Future of Arms Control," *Survival* 60, no. 2 (March/April 2018): 45–54.

[15] For assessments of Chinese perceptions of escalation risks, see Cunningham and Fravel, "Assuring Assured Retaliation," pp. 35–38, 40–41; and Talmadge, "Would China Go Nuclear?" pp. 51, 88–90.

[16] Thomas J. Christensen, "The Meaning of the Nuclear Evolution: China's Strategic Modernization and US-China Security Relations," *Journal of Strategic Studies* 35, no. 4 (August 2012): 447–87.

[17] Glenn A. Kent and David E. Thaler, *First-Strike Stability: A Methodology for Evaluating Strategic Forces* (Santa Monica, CA: RAND Corporation, 1989), p. 5, https://www.rand.org/pubs/reports/R3765.html. Also see Paul K. Davis, *Studying First-Strike Stability with Knowledge-Based Models of Human Decisionmaking* (Santa Monica, CA: RAND Corporation, 1989), https://www.rand.org/pubs/reports/R3689.html.

[18] Robert Jervis, *The Meaning of the Nuclear Revolution: Statecraft and the Prospect of Armageddon* (Ithaca, NY: Cornell University Press, 1989); and Schelling, *The Strategy of Conflict*.

[19] See discussion in Kent and Thaler, *First-Strike Stability*. Also see Brendan Rittenhouse Green et al., "Correspondence: The Limits of Damage Limitation," *International Security* 42, no. 1 (Summer 2017): 193–99.

[20] U.S. Department of Defense, *Nuclear Targeting Policy Review* (Washington: Department of Defense, November 1978), p. iv, https://www.archives.gov/files/declassification/iscap/pdf/2010 -079-doc1.pdf. Emphasis in original.

[21] See Glaser and Fetter, "Should the United States Reject MAD?," especially pp. 92–97.

[22] U.S. Department of Defense, *Nuclear Targeting Policy Review*, p. v. Emphasis in original.

[23] Brendan R. Green and Austin Long, "The MAD Who Wasn't There: Soviet Reactions to the Late Cold War Nuclear Balance," *Security Studies* 26, no. 4 (2017): 606–41. Also see Green et al., "Correspondence," pp. 193–207.

24 Svetlana Savranskaya and David A. Welch, "SALT II and the Growth of Mistrust: Transcript of the Proceedings of the Musgrove Conference of the Carter-Brezhnev Project" (Conference transcript, Musgrove, Simons Island, GA, May 1994), p. 24. This comment was relayed by Sergei Tarasenko, former aide to Soviet Foreign Minister Eduard Shevardnadze.

25 "Stasi Note on Meeting between Minister Mielke and KGB Chairman Andropov," July 11, 1981, History and Public Policy Program Digital Archive, Office of the Federal Commissioner for the Stasi Records (BStU), MfS, ZAIG 5382, p. 5, https://digitalarchive.wilsoncenter.org/document/115717.pdf?v=71c2f08516ef8a7ad53261324afc44d6. Translated from German for CWIHP by Bernd Schaefer. Emphasis in original.

26 President's Foreign Intelligence Advisory Board, *The Soviet "War Scare"* (Washington: President's Foreign Intelligence Advisory Board, February 15, 1990), https://nsarchive2.gwu.edu/nukevault/ebb533-The -Able-Archer-War-Scare-Declassified-PFIAB-Report-Released/2012 -0238-MR.pdf. The document is now declassified. Also see Marc Ambinder, *The Brink: President Reagan and the Nuclear War Scare of 1983* (New York: Simon and Schuster, 2018); and Benjamin Fischer, "Scolding Intelligence: The PFIAB Report on the Soviet War Scare," *International Journal of Intelligence and Counterintelligence* 31, no. 1 (2018): 102–15.

27 Matthew Kroenig, *The Logic of American Nuclear Strategy: Why Strategic Superiority Matters* (New York: Oxford University Press, 2018).

28 Keir Lieber and Daryl Press, "The New Era of Counterforce: Technological Change and the Future of Nuclear Deterrence," *International Security* 41, no. 4 (Spring 2017): 9–49; and Austin Long and Brendan Rittenhouse Green, "Stalking the Secure Second Strike: Intelligence, Counterforce, and Nuclear Strategy," *Journal of Strategic Studies* 38, nos. 1–2 (2015): 38–73.

29 Fiona Cunningham, "Maximizing Leverage: Explaining China's Strategic Force Postures in Limited Wars" (PhD thesis, Massachusetts Institute of Technology, 2018); and Green et al., "Correspondence."

30 James R. Schlesinger, *Some Notes on Deterrence in Western Europe* (Santa Monica, CA: RAND Corporation, 1962), p. 10.

31 Kent and Thaler, *First-Strike Stability*, p. 5.

32 For some of the reasons behind the difficulty of engaging the Chinese on these issues, see Oriana Mastro, "The Vulnerability of Rising Powers: The Logic Behind China's Low Military Transparency," *Asian Security* 12, no. 2 (2016): 63–81.

33 See Stephen Biddle and Ivan Oelrich, "Future Warfare in the Western Pacific: Chinese Antiaccess/Area Denial, U.S. AirSea Battle, and Command of the Commons in East Asia," *International Security* 41, no. 1 (2016): 7–48.

34 Office of the Secretary of Defense, *Summary of the 2018 National Defense Strategy of the United States of America*, p. 1.

35 Office of the Secretary of Defense, *Nuclear Posture Review 2018*, p. 23.

36 For more detailed discussion of these capabilities, see Paul Bracken, "The Cyber Threat to Nuclear Stability," *Orbis* 60, no. 2 (2016): 188–203; Lieber and Press, "The New Era of Counterforce," pp. 32–38; and Long and Green, "Stalking the Secure Second Strike," pp. 60–65.

Chapter 6

1 For summaries of the history of U.S. extended deterrence, see Steven Pifer et al., *U.S. Nuclear and Extended Deterrence: Considerations and Challenges* (Washington: Brookings Institution, May 2010), pp. 4–7, https://www.brookings.edu/wp-content/uploads/2016/06/06_nuclear_deterrence.pdf; Terence Roehrig, *Japan, South Korea, and the United States Nuclear Umbrella: Deterrence after the Cold War* (New York: Columbia University Press, 2017), pp. 38–63; and David J. Trachtenberg, "U.S. Extended Deterrence: How Much Strategic Force Is Too Little?," *Strategic Studies Quarterly* 6, no. 2 (Summer 2012): 65–67.

2 Office of the Secretary of Defense, *Summary of the 2018 National Defense Strategy of the United States of America: Sharpening the American Military's Competitive Edge* (Washington: Department of Defense, 2018), p. 1, https://www.defense.gov/Portals/1/Documents/pubs/2018-National-Defense-Strategy-Summary.pdf. Emphasis in original.

3 Julian Borger, "U.S. and Russia in Danger of Returning to Era of Nuclear Rivalry," *Guardian* (UK), January 4, 2015, https://www.theguardian.com/world/2015/jan/04/us-russia-era-nuclear-rivalry; Bob Davis, "U.S. Unveils Additional Tariffs on $200 Billion

More in Chinese Imports," *Wall Street Journal*, July 10, 2018, https://www.wsj.com/articles/u-s-preparingadditionaltariffs-onup-to-200-billionof-chinese-imports-1531260864; Marco Rubio, "To Fight China on Trade, We Need More than Tariffs," *New York Times*, March 13, 2018, https://www.nytimes.com/2018/03/13/opinion/rubio-china-trade-tariffs.html; and Christopher Wray, "China Is 'Most Challenging' Threat the U.S. Faces, FBI Director Says," interview by Lester Holt, NBC News, July 18, 2018, https://www.nbcnews.com/nightly-news/video/china-is-most-challenging-threat-the-u-s-faces-fbi-director-says-1280700995803.

4 Office of the Secretary of Defense, *Nuclear Posture Review 2018* (Washington: Department of Defense, February 2018), pp. 8–11, https://media.defense.gov/2018/Feb/02/2001872886/-1/-1/1/2018-NUCLEAR-POSTURE-REVIEW-FINAL-REPORT.PDF.

5 For a summary of China's path to nuclear weapons, see John Wilson Lewis and Xue Litai, *China Builds the Bomb* (Stanford, CA: Stanford University Press, 1988). For a discussion of China's nuclear modernization effort, see Fiona S. Cunningham and M. Taylor Fravel, "Assuring Assured Retaliation: China's Nuclear Posture and U.S.-China Strategic Stability," *International Security* 40, no. 2 (Fall 2015): 14–15; and Jeffrey Lewis, "China's Nuclear Modernization: Surprise, Restraint and Uncertainty," in *Strategic Asia 2013–14: Asia in the Second Nuclear Age*, ed. Ashley J. Tellis, Abraham Denmark, and Travis Tanner (Seattle, WA: National Bureau of Asian Research, 2013), pp. 71–74.

6 Lyle J. Goldstein, "When China Was a 'Rogue State': The Impact of China's Nuclear Weapons Program on US-China Relations during the 1960s," *Journal of Contemporary China* 12, no. 37 (2003): 739–64.

7 Eric Heginbotham et al., *The U.S.-China Military Scorecard: Forces, Geography, and the Evolving Balance of Power 1996–2017* (Santa Monica, CA: RAND Corporation, 2015).

8 Lim Yan Liang, "NPC 2018: China Raises Military Budget by 8.1% in Face of 'Profound Changes' to National Security Environment," *Straits Times* (Singapore), March 5, 2018, https://www.straitstimes.com/asia/east-asia/china-raises-2018-defence-spending-by-81-per-cent; and Joel Wuthnow and Phillip C. Saunders, *Chinese Military*

Reforms in the Age of Xi Jinping (Washington: National Defense University Press, March 2017), http://ndupress.ndu.edu/Portals/68/Documents/stratperspective/china/ChinaPerspectives-10.pdf.

9   Joshua R. Itzkowitz Shifrinson, "Deal or No Deal? The End of the Cold War and the U.S. Offer to Limit NATO Expansion," *International Security* 40, no. 4 (Spring 2016): 7–44.

10 Kristin Ven Bruusgaard, "Russian Strategic Deterrence," *Survival* 58, no. 4 (2016): 7–26; Michael Kofman, "Fixing NATO Deterrence in the East or: How I Learned to Stop Worrying and Love NATO's Crushing Defeat by Russia," War on the Rocks, May 12, 2016, https://warontherocks.com/2016/05/fixing-nato-deterrence-in-the-east-or-how-i-learned-to-stop-worrying-and-love-natos-crushing-defeat-by-russia/; and Michael Kofman, "Russian Performance in the Russo-Georgian War Revisited," War on the Rocks, September 4, 2018, https://warontherocks.com/2018/09/russian-performance-in-the-russo-georgian-war-revisited/.

11 Data obtained from https://data.worldbank.org/indicator/NY.GDP.MKTP.CD?end=2017&start=1997&view=chart&year_high_desc=true.

12 On the "unipolar moment," see Charles Krauthammer, "The Unipolar Moment," *Foreign Affairs* 70, no. 1 (Winter 1990), https://www.foreignaffairs.com/articles/1991-02-01/unipolar-moment.

13 Matthew Kroenig, *The Logic of American Nuclear Strategy: Why Strategic Superiority Matters* (New York: Oxford University Press, 2018).

14 Office of the Secretary of Defense, *Nuclear Posture Review 2018*, p. 30.

15 Elbridge Colby, "If You Want Peace, Prepare for Nuclear War," *Foreign Affairs*, October 15, 2018, https://www.foreignaffairs.com/articles/china/2018-10-15/if-you-want-peace-prepare-nuclear-war; and Keith B. Payne, "Why U.S. Nuclear Force Numbers Matter," *Strategic Studies Quarterly* 10, no. 2 (Summer 2016): 18–19.

16 Jonathan Cheng and Farnaz Fassihi, "U.S. Opens Way to Boost Arms Sales to Asia Allies," *Wall Street Journal*, September 5, 2017, https://www.wsj.com/articles/north-korea-crisis-strengthens-alliances-u-s-naval-commander-says-1504605651; Benjamin H. Friedman and Joshua Shifrinson, "Trump, NATO, and Establishment Hysteria,"

War on the Rocks, June 16, 2017, https://warontherocks.com/2017/06
/trump-nato-and-establishment-hysteria/; and Jen Judson, "Funding to Deter Russia Reaches $6.5B in FY19 Defense Budget Request,"
Defense News, February 12, 2018, https://www.defensenews.com
/land/2018/02/12/funding-to-deter-russia-reaches-65b-in-fy19
-defense-budget-request/.

[17] Payne, "Why U.S. Nuclear Force Numbers Matter," p. 19.

[18] Eric Gomez, "Nuclear Umbrella or Nuclear Albatross?," in "Book
Review Roundtable: The Future of Extended Deterrence," *Texas National
Security Review*, February 28, 2018, https://tnsr.org/roundtable/book
-review-roundtable-future-extended-deterrence/#essay2; and Roehrig,
Japan, South Korea, and the United States Nuclear Umbrella, p. 187.

[19] Roehrig, *Japan, South Korea, and the United States Nuclear Umbrella*,
p. 111. Emphasis added.

[20] Ben Brimelow, "Pentagon Warns that the US Is Falling Behind to
China in Hypersonic Missile Race," *Business Insider*, April 20, 2018,
https://www.businessinsider.com/us-falling-behind-to-china
-hypersonic-missile-race-2018-4; Ryan Evans et al., "Policy Roundtable:
A Close Look at the 2018 National Defense Strategy," *Texas National
Security Review*, January 26, 2018, https://tnsr.org/roundtable/policy
-roundtable-close-look-2018-national-defense-strategy/#essay5; and
Michael Pence, "Remarks by Vice President Pence on the Future of the
U.S. Military in Space" (speech at the Pentagon, August 9, 2018), The
White House, https://www.whitehouse.gov/briefings-statements
/remarks-vice-president-pence-future-u-s-military-space/.

[21] Office of the Secretary of Defense, *Nuclear Posture Review 2018*, p. 2.

[22] Office of the Secretary of Defense, *Nuclear Posture Review 2018*, pp. 21,
54–55.

[23] Todd S. Sechser and Matthew Fuhrmann, *Nuclear Weapons and Coercive
Diplomacy* (Cambridge: Cambridge University Press, 2017), pp. 17–19.

[24] Jasen J. Castillo and John V. Parachini, "Assessing Nuclear Escalation
in Conventional Conflicts: Implications for Intelligence Analysis and
Tasking" (unpublished paper, October 2017), pp. 29–30; and Forrest
E. Morgan et al., *Dangerous Thresholds: Managing Escalation in the 21st
Century* (Santa Monica, CA: RAND Corporation, 2008), pp. xiii, 34–35.

25 The ability of the United States to hold Russian and Chinese nuclear forces at risk is a matter of debate among academic experts. See Charles L. Glaser and Steve Fetter, "Should the United States Reject MAD? Damage Limitation and U.S. Nuclear Strategy toward China," *International Security* 41, no. 1 (Summer 2016): 49–98; Brendan Rittenhouse Green et al., "Correspondence: The Limits of Damage Limitation," *International Security* 42, no. 1 (Summer 2017): 193–99; and Austin Long and Brendan Rittenhouse Green, "Stalking the Secure Second Strike: Intelligence, Counterforce, and Nuclear Strategy," *Journal of Strategic Studies* 38, nos. 1–2 (2015): 38–73.

26 Castillo and Parachini, "Assessing Nuclear Escalation in Conventional Conflicts," p. 30; Caitlin Talmadge, "Would China Go Nuclear? Assessing the Risk of Chinese Nuclear Escalation in a Conventional War with the United States," *International Security* 41, no. 4 (Spring 2017): 65–84; and Joshua Rovner, "Two Kinds of Catastrophe: Nuclear Escalation and Protracted War in Asia," *Journal of Strategic Studies* 40, no. 5 (2017): 7–9.

27 James M. Acton, "Escalation through Entanglement: How the Vulnerability of Command-and-Control Systems Raises the Risks of an Inadvertent Nuclear War," *International Security* 43, no. 1 (Summer 2018): 67–82.

28 Acton, "Escalation through Entanglement," pp. 61–66. Also see Tong Zhao and Li Bin, "The Underappreciated Risks of Entanglement: A Chinese Perspective," in *Entanglement: Russian and Chinese Perspectives on Non-Nuclear Weapons and Nuclear Risks*, ed. James M. Acton (Washington: Carnegie Endowment for International Peace, 2017), pp. 52–53, 58–59.

29 Devlin Barrett, Danny Yadron, and Damian Paletta, "U.S. Suspects Hackers in China Breached about 4 Million People's Records, Officials Say," *Wall Street Journal*, June 5, 2015, https://www.wsj.com/articles/u-s-suspects-hackers-in-china-behind-government-data-breach-sources-say-1433451888; Mark Mazzetti and Katie Benner, "12 Russian Agents Indicted in Mueller Investigation," *New York Times*, July 13, 2018, https://www.nytimes.com/2018/07/13/us/politics/mueller-indictment-russian-intelligence-hacking.html;

and Everett Rosenfeld, "U.S.-China Agree to Not Conduct Cybertheft of Intellectual Property," CNBC, September 25, 2015, https://www.cnbc.com/2015/09/25/us-china-agree-to-not-conduct-cybertheft-of-intellectual-property-white-house.html.

[30] Steven Lee Myers, "With Ships and Missiles, China Is Ready to Challenge U.S. Navy in Pacific," *New York Times*, August 29, 2018, https://www.nytimes.com/2018/08/29/world/asia/china-navy-aircraft-carrier-pacific.html.

[31] The transformative effect of nuclear weapons on international relations is known as the "nuclear revolution." See Robert Jervis, *The Meaning of the Nuclear Revolution: Statecraft and the Prospect of Armageddon* (Ithaca, NY: Cornell University Press, 1989).

[32] Robert Jervis, "Cooperation under the Security Dilemma," *World Politics* 30, no. 2 (January 1978): 187–99.

[33] Michael S. Gerson, "Conventional Deterrence in the Second Nuclear Age," *Parameters* (Autumn 2009): 37–38.

[34] On the continued importance of nuclear weapons in extended deterrence, see Roehrig, *Japan, South Korea, and the United States Nuclear Umbrella*, p. 10. On the relative value of nuclear and conventional systems for extended deterrence, see Gomez, "Nuclear Umbrella or Nuclear Albatross?"

[35] Thomas C. Schelling, *Arms and Influence*, 2008 edition (New Haven, CT: Yale University Press, 2008 [1966]), p. 36.

[36] Ivan Arreguín-Toft, *How the Weak Win Wars: A Theory of Asymmetric Conflict* (Cambridge: Cambridge University Press, 2005).

[37] Cunningham and Fravel, "Assuring Assured Retaliation," p. 35.

[38] Acton, "Escalation through Entanglement," p. 66; Stephen Biddle and Ivan Oelrich, "Future Warfare in the Western Pacific: Chinese Antiaccess/Area Denial, U.S. AirSea Battle, and Command of the Commons in East Asia," *International Security* 41, no.1 (Summer 2016): 8–10; and Talmadge, "Would China Go Nuclear?," p. 53.

[39] On the situational awareness requirements for modern, complex conventional warfare, see Biddle and Oelrich, "Future Warfare in the Western Pacific," pp. 22–30; and Kofman, "Russian Performance in the Russo-Georgian War Revisited."

40 Acton, "Escalation through Entanglement," pp. 56–99; Talmadge, "Would China Go Nuclear?" pp. 53, 55, 57, 62.

41 Multiple studies examine what allied A2/AD could look like. For example, Michael Beckley, "The Emerging Balance in East Asia: How China's Neighbors Can Check Chinese Naval Expansion," *International Security* 42, no. 2 (Fall 2017): 78–119; Timothy M. Bonds, *What Role Can Land-Based, Multi-Domain Anti-Access/Area Denial Forces Play in Deterring or Defeating Aggression?* (Santa Monica, CA: RAND Corporation, 2017); and Jim Thomas, Iskander Rehman, and John Stillion, *Hard ROC 2.0: Taiwan and Deterrence through Protraction* (Washington: Center for Strategic and Budgetary Assessments, December 2014).

42 Eric Heginbotham and Richard J. Samuels, "Active Denial: Redesigning Japan's Response to China's Military Challenge," *International Security* 42, no. 4 (Spring 2018): 153–56.

Chapter 7

1 Hans M. Kristensen and Robert S. Norris, "North Korean Nuclear Capabilities, 2018," *Bulletin of the Atomic Scientists* 74, no. 1 (2018): 41–51.

2 David Wright, "North Korea's Longest Missile Test Yet," *All Things Nuclear*, Union of Concerned Scientists, November 28, 2017, https://allthingsnuclear.org/dwright/nk-longest-missile-test-yet.

3 Alexandre Y. Mansourov, "Kim Jong Un's Nuclear Doctrine and Strategy: What Everyone Needs to Know," *NAPSNet Special Report*, Nautilus Institute, December 16, 2014, https://nautilus.org/napsnet/napsnet-special-reports/kim-jong-uns-nuclear-doctrine-and-strategy-what-everyone-needs-to-know/.

4 Former National Security Advisor H. R. McMaster made this argument during his time in the White House. See James Jeffrey, "What If H. R. McMaster Is Right about North Korea?" *The Atlantic*, January 18, 2018, https://www.theatlantic.com/international/archive/2018/01/hr-mcmaster-might-be-right-about-north-korea/550799/.

5 Mike Pompeo, interview by Marc A. Thiessen, "Intelligence beyond 2018: A Conversation with CIA Director Mike Pompeo," American

Enterprise Institute, January 23, 2018, https://www.aei.org/events /intelligence-beyond-2018-a-conversation-with-cia-director-mike -pompeo-livestreamed-event/.

6 Quoted in Kenneth M. Pollack, *Unthinkable: Iran, the Bomb, and American Strategy* (New York: Simon and Schuster, 2013), p. 78.

7 Eric S. Edelman and Whitney Morgan McNamara, *Contain, Degrade, and Defeat: A Defense Strategy for a Troubled Middle East* (Washington: Center for Strategic and Budgetary Assessments, 2017), pp. 28–29.

8 Robert A. Pape, *Bombing to Win: Air Power and Coercion in War* (Ithaca, NY: Cornell University Press, 1996), p. 38. Other examples of the coercionist school include Kyle Beardsley and Victor Asal, "Winning with the Bomb," *Journal of Conflict Resolution* 53, no. 2 (2009): 278–301; John Merrill and Ilan Peleg, "Nuclear Compellence: The Political Use of the Bomb," *Crossroads* 11 (1984): 19–39; and Bradley A. Thayer and Thomas M. Skypek, "Reaffirming the Utility of Nuclear Weapons," *Parameters* 42, no. 4 (2013): 41–45.

9 Harry S. Truman, *Memoirs by Harry S. Truman, Vol. 1: Year of Decisions* (Garden City, NY: Doubleday and Company, 1955), p. 87.

10 U.S. Department of Defense, Office of International Security Affairs, "China as a Nuclear Power (Some Thoughts prior to the Chinese Test)," October 7, 1964, p. 4. Declassified under the Freedom of Information Act.

11 First quotation in Keith B. Payne, "Nuclear Deterrence in a New Age," *Comparative Strategy* 37, no. 1 (2018): 4. Second quotation in David E. Sanger, "Suppose We Just Let Iran Have the Bomb," *New York Times*, March 19, 2006, https://www.nytimes.com/2006/03/19 /weekinreview/suppose-we-just-let-iran-have-the-bomb.html.

12 For example, see John Bolton, "The Legal Case for Striking North Korea First," *Wall Street Journal*, February 28, 2018, https://www.wsj .com/articles/the-legal-case-for-striking-north-korea-first-1519862374; Edward Luttwak, "It's Time to Bomb North Korea," *Foreign Policy*, January 8, 2018, https://foreignpolicy.com/2018/01/08/its-time-to -bomb-north-korea/; and Crispin Rovere, "The Case for War with North Korea," *The National Interest*, July 11, 2017, https://nationalinterest.org /blog/the-buzz/the-case-war-north-korea-21500.

13 Carl von Clausewitz, *On War*, ed. and trans. Michael Howard and Peter Paret (Princeton, NJ: Princeton University Press, 1976 [1832]), p. 370.

14 See Thomas C. Schelling, *Arms and Influence* (New Haven, CT: Yale University Press, 1966), pp. 69–91.

15 Todd S. Sechser and Matthew Fuhrmann, *Nuclear Weapons and Coercive Diplomacy* (Cambridge: Cambridge University Press, 2017).

16 Todd S. Sechser, "Militarized Compellent Threats, 1918–2001," *Conflict Management and Peace Science* 28, no. 4 (2011): 377–401.

17 Sechser and Fuhrmann, *Nuclear Weapons and Coercive Diplomacy*, pp. 84–85. The overall result remains similar if we loosen the definition of a successful compellent threat; see Todd S. Sechser and Matthew Fuhrmann, "The Madman and the Bomb: Nuclear Blackmail in the Trump Era," *Virginia Policy Review* 10, no. 2 (2017): 81–87.

18 For a separate article, we repeated these tests using several different definitions of nuclear "superiority," but the findings were the same. See Todd S. Sechser and Matthew Fuhrmann, "Crisis Bargaining and Nuclear Blackmail," *International Organization* 67, no. 1 (2013): 173–95.

19 Acquiring long-range ballistic missiles, as North Korea appears to have done, has not historically improved coercive outcomes. See Todd S. Sechser, "Reputations and Signaling in Coercive Bargaining," *Journal of Conflict Resolution* 62, no. 2 (2018): 318–45.

20 We elaborate on these and other potential costs in Sechser and Fuhrmann, *Nuclear Weapons and Coercive Diplomacy*, pp. 48–50.

21 Paul K. Huth and Todd L. Allee, *The Democratic Peace and Territorial Conflict in the Twentieth Century* (New York: Cambridge University Press, 2002).

22 See, for example, S. Paul Kapur, *Dangerous Deterrent: Nuclear Weapons Proliferation and Conflict in South Asia* (Palo Alto, CA: Stanford University Press, 2007).

23 Colin H. Kahl and Kenneth N. Waltz, "Iran and the Bomb: Would a Nuclear Iran Make the Middle East More Secure?" *Foreign Affairs* 91, no. 5 (2012): 158.

24 Robert M. Danin, "Iran with the Bomb," in *Iran: The Nuclear Challenge*, ed. Robert D. Blackwill (New York: Council on Foreign Relations, 2012).

[25] For example, see Suzanne Maloney, "Thinking the Unthinkable: The Gulf States and the Prospect of a Nuclear Iran," Middle East Memo no. 27 (Washington: Brookings Institution, January 2013), https://www.brookings.edu/research/thinking-the-unthinkable-the-gulf-states-and-the-prospect-of-a-nuclear-iran/.

[26] Quoted in Sechser and Fuhrmann, *Nuclear Weapons and Coercive Diplomacy*, p. 207.

[27] The United States promised not to invade Cuba in exchange for the removal of the Soviet missiles. In addition, Khrushchev privately obtained a second concession from the United States—namely, the agreement to withdraw nuclear missiles from Turkey.

[28] Michael C. Horowitz, "The Spread of Nuclear Weapons and International Conflict: Does Experience Matter?" *Journal of Conflict Resolution* 53, no. 2 (2009): 234–57.

[29] Matthew Fuhrmann and Sarah E. Kreps, "Targeting Nuclear Programs in War and Peace: A Quantitative Empirical Analysis, 1941–2000," *Journal of Conflict Resolution* 54, no. 6 (2010): 831–59.

[30] John R. Bolton, "To Stop Iran's Bomb, Bomb Iran," *New York Times*, March 26, 2015, https://www.nytimes.com/2015/03/26/opinion/to-stop-irans-bomb-bomb-iran.html.

[31] Donald J. Trump, Twitter post, July 22, 2018, 8:24 p.m., https://twitter.com/realdonaldtrump/status/1021234525626609666. All caps in original.

[32] Noah Bierman, "Trump Warns North Korea of 'Fire and Fury,'" *Los Angeles Times*, August 8, 2017, http://www.latimes.com/politics/washington/la-na-essential-washington-updates-trump-warns-north-korea-of-fire-and-1502220642-htmlstory.html.

[33] The full text of the statement can be found online at https://www.whitehouse.gov/briefings-statements/joint-statement-president-donald-j-trump-united-states-america-chairman-kim-jong-un-democratic-peoples-republic-korea-singapore-summit/.

[34] Choe Sang-Hun, "North Korea Starts Dismantling Key Missile Facilities, Report Says," *New York Times*, July 23, 2018, https://www.nytimes.com/2018/07/23/world/asia/north-korea-dismantling-missile-facilities.html.

35 Norman Podhoretz, "The Case for Bombing Iran," *Commentary*, June 1, 2007, https://www.commentarymagazine.com/articles/the -case-for-bombing-iran/.

36 For further details on the challenges the United States would face in using preventive war threats to limit or roll back nuclear programs in Iran and North Korea, see Matthew Fuhrmann, "When Preventive War Threats Work for Nuclear Nonproliferation," *Washington Quarterly* 41, no. 3 (2018): 111–35.

Chapter 8

1 Heather Nauert, "Trump Administration INF Treaty Integrated Strategy," press release, U.S. Department of State, December 8, 2017, https://www.state.gov/trump-administration-inf-treaty-integrated -strategy/.

2 The full text of the JCPOA can be found here, http://www.europarl .europa.eu/cmsdata/122460/full-text-of-the-iran-nuclear-deal.pdf.

3 This relief included lifting provisions of (a) previous UN Security Council resolutions on Iran, (b) U.S. and E.U. nuclear-related sanctions, and (c) the U.S. trade ban on certain imports and exports.

4 Donald Trump, "Remarks by President Trump on the Joint Comprehensive Plan of Action," (speech, White House, Washington, May 8, 2018), https://www.whitehouse.gov/briefings-statements/remarks -president-trump-joint-comprehensive-plan-action/.

5 "Frequently Asked Questions Regarding the Re-Imposition of Sanctions Pursuant to the May 8, 2018, National Security Presidential Memorandum Relating to the Joint Comprehensive Plan of Action (JCPOA)," U.S. Department of the Treasury, August 6, 2018, https://www.treasury.gov/resource-center/sanctions/Programs /Documents/jcpoa_winddown_faqs.pdf; "Trump Administration to Reinstate All Iran Sanctions," BBC News, November 3, 2018, https:// www.bbc.com/news/world-us-canada-46071747; and Sergio R. Bustos, "U.S.-Imposed Sanctions on Iranian Oil Industry Will 'Cripple' Iran's Economy, Report Says," *USA Today*, August 29, 2018, https://www .usatoday.com/story/news/world/2018/08/29/trump-sanctions-oil -industry-cripple-irans-economy-report/1132277002/.

6   Michael R. Pompeo, "Confronting Iran: The Trump Administration's Strategy," *Foreign Affairs* 97, no. 6 (November / December 2018), https:/ / www.foreignaffairs.com / articles / middle-east / 2018-10-15 / michael-pompeo-secretary-of-state-on-confronting-iran.

7   Bureau of Arms Control, Verification, and Compliance, *Adherence to and Compliance with Arms Control, Nonproliferation, and Disarmament Agreements and Commitments* (Washington: U.S. Department of State, April 2018), pp. 22–23, https:/ / www.state.gov / 2018-report-on -adherence-to-and-compliance-with-arms-control-nonproliferation -and-disarmament-agreements-and-commitments / .

8   Daniel R. Coats, "Worldwide Threat Assessment of the US Intelligence Community," statement for the record, Senate Select Committee on Intelligence, January 29, 2019, p. 10, https:/ / www .intelligence.senate.gov / sites / default / files / documents / os-dcoats -012919.pdf.

9   Melissa De Witte and Katy Gabel, "Stanford Scholars Weigh In on Withdrawal from the Iran Nuclear Deal," Stanford News Service, May 8, 2018, https:/ / news.stanford.edu / press-releases / 2018 / 05 / 08 / stanford-scholardrawal-iran-deal / .

10 "Russia Voices 'Unconditional' Support for Iran Nuclear Deal," Moscow Times, September 25, 2018, https:/ / themoscowtimes.com / news /; and Samantha Pitz and Ryan Fedasiuk, "International Support for the Iran Nuclear Deal," Arms Control NOW blog post, Arms Control Association, May 9, 2018, https:/ / www.armscontrol.org / blog / 2018-05-09 / international-support-iran-nuclear-deal.

11 Dalia Dassa Kaye, "The Strategic Fallout of U.S. Withdrawal from the Iran Deal," The RAND Blog, RAND Corporation, May 10, 2018, https:/ / www.rand.org / blog / 2018 / 05 / the-strategic-fallout-of-us -withdrawal-from-the-iran.html.

12 Kaye, "The Strategic Fallout of U.S. Withdrawal from the Iran Deal."

13 Carol Morello, "Iran Plans New Uranium Enrichment," *Washington Post*, June 5, 2018, https:/ / www.washingtonpost.com / world / national -security / iran-plans-new-uranium-enrichment / 2018 / 06 / 05 / 22cc5142 -68fd-11e8-bf8c-f9ed2e672adf_story.html?utm_term=.d160a48d5d34.

[14] "Iran Completes Facility to Build Centrifuges: Nuclear Chief," Reuters, September 9, 2018, https://www.reuters.com/article/us-iran-nuclear-salehi/iran-completes-facility-to-build-centrifuges-nuclear-chief-idUSKCN1LP0RE.

[15] On nuclear proliferation risks, see Nicole Gaouette, "Saudi Arabia Set to Pursue Nuclear Weapons if Iran Restarts Program," CNN, May 9, 2018, https://www.cnn.com/2018/05/09/politics/saudi-arabia-nuclear-weapons/index.html; and David E. Sanger and William J. Broad, "Saudis Want a U.S. Nuclear Deal. Can They Be Trusted Not to Build a Bomb?" *New York Times*, November 22, 2018, https://www.nytimes.com/2018/11/22/world/middleeast/saudi-arabia-nuclear.html. On preemptive action, see Louis Rene Beres, "Israel's Nuclear Strategy after the Iran Agreement," *The Hill*, July 22, 2015, https://thehill.com/blogs/pundits-blog/international/248765-israels-nuclear-strategy-after-the-iran-agreement; and Amos Harel and Aluf Benn, "No Longer a Secret: How Israel Destroyed Syria's Nuclear Reactor," *Haaretz*, March 23, 2018, https://www.haaretz.com/world-news/MAGAZINE-no-longer-a-secret-how-israel-destroyed-syria-s-nuclear-reactor-1.5914407.

[16] "Iran Nuclear Deal: Khamenei Lists Demands for European Powers," BBC News, May 23, 2018, https://www.bbc.com/news/world-middle-east-44230983.

[17] Mike Pompeo, "After the Deal: A New Iran Strategy" (speech, Heritage Foundation, Washington, May 21, 2018), https://www.heritage.org/defense/event/after-the-deal-new-iran-strategy.

[18] Pompeo, "Confronting Iran."

[19] Suzanne Maloney, "Iran Isn't Taking Trump's Twitter Bait—for Now," *Atlantic*, July 25, 2018, https://www.theatlantic.com/international/archive/2018/07/trump-pressure-iran-rouhani/566000/.

[20] Ellie Geranmayeh and Esfandyar Batmanghelidj, "How Europe Can Block Trump," *Foreign Policy*, May 16, 2018, https://foreignpolicy.com/2018/05/16/how-europe-can-block-trump/.

[21] "Iran Completes Facility to Build Centrifuges," Reuters.

[22] Kenneth Katzman, Paul K. Kerr, and Valerie Heitshusen, *U.S. Decision to Cease Implementing the Iran Nuclear Agreement*, CRS Report

R44942 (Washington: Congressional Research Service, May 9, 2018), p. i, https://fas.org/sgp/crs/nuke/R44942.pdf.

23 Natasha Turak, "Europe, Russia, and China Join Forces with a New Mechanism to Dodge Iran Sanctions," CNBC, September 25, 2018, https://www.cnbc.com/2018/09/25/eu-russia-and-china-join-forces-to-dodge-iran-sanctions.html.

24 Quote from Ellie Geranmayeh and Esfandyar Batmanghelidj, "Trading with Iran Via the Special Purpose Vehicle: How It Can Work," European Council on Foreign Relations, February 7, 2019, https://www.ecfr.eu/article/commentary_trading_with_iran_special_purpose_vehicle_how_it_can_work. Also see Jean-Yves Le Drian, Heiko Maas, and Jeremy Hunt, "Joint Statement [by the E3 Foreign Ministers] on the Creation of INSTEX, the Special Purpose Vehicle Aimed at Facilitating Legitimate Trade with Iran in the Framework of the Efforts to Preserve the Joint Comprehensive Plan of Action (JCPOA)," France Diplomatie, January 31, 2019, https://www.diplomatie.gouv.fr/en/country-files/iran/events/article/joint-statement-on-the-creation-of-instex-the-special-purpose-vehicle-aimed-at.

25 Bureau of Arms Control, Verification, and Compliance, "Treaty between the United States of America and the Union of Soviet Socialist Republics on the Elimination of Their Intermediate-Range and Shorter-Range Missiles (INF Treaty)," U.S. Department of State, December 8, 1987, https://www.state.gov/t/avc/trty/102360.htm.

26 Terry Atlas and Maggie Tennis, "Russia Advances Banned Cruise Missile," *Arms Control Today*, March 2017, https://www.armscontrol.org/act/2017-03/news/russia-advances-banned-cruise-missile.

27 Robert M. Gates, *Duty: Memoirs of a Secretary at War* (New York: Alfred A. Knopf, 2014), p. 154.

28 Ankit Panda, "The Uncertain Future of the INF Treaty," Council on Foreign Relations, October 22, 2018, https://www.cfr.org/backgrounder/uncertain-future-inf-treaty; and Steven Pifer and Oliver Meier, "Are We Nearing the End of the INF Treaty?" *Arms Control Today*, January/February 2018, https://www.armscontrol.org/act/2018-01/features/we-nearing-end-inf-treaty.

29 Steven Pifer, "RIP INF: The End of a Landmark Treaty," Brookings Institution, November 1, 2018, https://www.brookings.edu/blog/order -from-chaos/2018/11/01/rip-inf-the-end-of-a-landmark-treaty/.

30 Pifer and Meier, "Are We Nearing the End of the INF Treaty?"

31 Bureau of Arms Control, Verification, and Compliance, "Refuting Russian Allegations of U.S. Noncompliance with the INF Treaty," fact sheet, U.S. Department of State, December 8, 2017, https://www .state.gov/refuting-russian-allegations-of-u-s-noncompliance-with -the-inf-treaty/.

32 "President Donald J. Trump Is Standing Up to Russia's Malign Activities," fact sheet, The White House, April 6, 2018, https://www .whitehouse.gov/briefings-statements/president-donald-j-trump -standing-russias-malign-activities/; Nauert, "Trump Administration INF Treaty Integrated Strategy;" and Office of the Secretary of Defense, *Nuclear Posture Review 2018* (Washington: U.S. Department of Defense, February 2018), p. 10, https://media.defense.gov/2018 /Feb/02/2001872886/-1/-1/1/2018-NUCLEAR-POSTURE-REVIEW -FINAL-REPORT.PDF.

33 Sophie Tatum, Ryan Browne, and Kevin Bohn, "Trump Says U.S. Is Ending Decades-Old Nuclear Arms Treaty with Russia," CNN, October 21, 2018, https://www.cnn.com/2018/10/20/politics /donald-trump-us-arms-agreement-russia/index.html.

34 Editorial Board, "The Trump Administration Says It Will Walk Away from a Nuclear Treaty. Then What?" *Washington Post*, December 9, 2018, https://www.washingtonpost.com/opinions/the -trump-administration-says-it-will-walk-away-from-a-nuclear-treaty -then-what/2018/12/09/07eec646-f8d8-11e8-8d64-4e79db33382f _story.html?utm_term=.e0a9cc637726.

35 Aaron Mehta, "The U.S. Has Taken the First Step to Leaving an Arms Control Treaty. What Happens Next?" *Defense News*, December 4, 2018, https://www.defensenews.com/smr/nuclear-arsenal/2018/12/04 /pompeo-us-will-leave-nuclear-treaty-over-russian-cheating/.

36 Michael R. Pompeo, "Remarks to the Press," U.S. Department of State, February 1, 2019, https://ru.usembassy.gov/remarks-by-michael -r-pompeo-remarks-to-the-press/.

[37] Vladimir Putin, "Meeting with Sergei Lavrov and Sergei Shoigu," President of Russia, February 2, 2019, http://en.kremlin.ru/events /president/news/59763.

[38] Jon Wolfsthal, "After Deployment: What? Russian Violations of the INF Treaty," Carnegie Endowment for International Peace, March 30, 2017, http://carnegieendowment.org/2017/03/30/after-deployment -what-russian-violations-of-inf-treaty-pub-68514.

[39] North Atlantic Treaty Organization, "Statement on the Intermediate-Range Nuclear Forces (INF) Treaty," press release, Brussels, Belgium, December 4, 2018, https://www.nato.int/cps/en/natohq/official _texts_161122.htm?selectedLocale=en.

[40] Amy Woolf, *Russian Compliance with the Intermediate Range Nuclear Forces (INF) Treaty: Background and Issues for Congress*, CRS Report R43832 (Washington: Congressional Research Service, February 8, 2019), p. 8, https://fas.org/sgp/crs/nuke/R43832.pdf.

[41] "Poland Supports U.S. Withdrawal from INF," DW [Deutsche Welle], October 25, 2018, https://www.dw.com/en/poland-supports-us -withdrawal-from-inf/a-46049028.

[42] Matt Korda and Hans M. Kristensen, "Trump Falls on Sword for Putin's Treaty Violation," Bulletin of the Atomic Scientists, October 29, 2018, https://thebulletin.org/2018/10/trump-falls-on-sword-for-putins -treaty-violation/.

[43] Tom Z. Collina, "Welcome to the New Nuclear Arms Race," *The Hill*, February 2, 2019, https://thehill.com/opinion/national-security /428327-welcome-to-the-new-nuclear-arms-race.

[44] These inspections would include displays of the Russian violating missile and the U.S. Aegis Ashore missile defense system to U.S. and Russian officials and experts. See Steven Pifer, "U.S. Response to Russian Treaty Violation Plays into Moscow's Hands," Order from Chaos blog post, Brookings Institution, November 15, 2017, https:// www.brookings.edu/blog/order-from-chaos/2017/11/15/u-s -response-to-russian-treaty-violation-plays-into-moscows-hands/; and Greg Thielmann and Andrei Zagorski, "INF Treaty Compliance: A Challenge and an Opportunity," Deep Cuts Working Paper no. 9,

February 2017, http://deepcuts.org/images/PDF/DeepCuts_WP9
_ThielmannZagorski.pdf.

45 "Deployed warheads" only refers to the number of warheads carried
by the delivery systems covered by New START, with heavy bombers counting as one deployed warhead, regardless of the number
of nuclear weapons that the bomber can carry at any one time. See
https://www.state.gov/new-start/.

46 On February 22, 2018, the U.S. State Department published a fact
sheet showing that the United States declared 1,350 deployed
warheads, 652 deployed delivery systems, and 800 deployed
and nondeployed delivery systems. Russia declared 1,444, 527,
and 779, respectively. See https://www.state.gov/new-start-treaty
-aggregate-numbers-of-strategic-offensive-arms-8/.

47 "New START Treaty Inspection Activities," U.S. Department of
State, December 13, 2018, https://www.state.gov/new-start-treaty
-inspection-activities/.

48 Steven Pifer, "New START at 7," Order from Chaos blog post, Brookings
Institution, February 5, 2018, https://www.brookings.edu/blog/order
-from-chaos/2018/02/05/new-start-at-7/.

49 Karen DeYoung, "Bolton and His Russian Counterpart Discuss
Arms Control, Syria and Iran," *Washington Post*, August 23, 2018,
https://www.washingtonpost.com/world/national-security/bolton
-and-his-russian-counterpart-discuss-arms-control-syria-and-iran
/2018/08/23/626eb772-a6f6-11e8-a656-943eefab5daf_story
.html?noredirect=on&utm_term=.1e92c3676d07.

50 John Bolton, "Former Ambassador John Bolton at 2017 Conservative
Political Action Conference" (speech, Conservative Political Action
Conference, February 24, 2017), C-SPAN, https://www.c-span.org
/video/?424395-9/ambassador-john-bolton-2017-conservative
-political-action-conference.

51 Frank Klotz, "Extending New START Is in America's National Security
Interest," *Arms Control Today*, January/February 2019, https://www
.armscontrol.org/act/2019-01/features/extending-new-start-americas
-national-security-interest.

52 See, for example, testimony of General John Hyten (commander, U.S. Strategic Command), Admiral Bill Moran (Vice Chief of Naval Operations), General Paul Selva (vice chairman, Joint Chiefs of Staff), and General Stephen Wilson (vice chief of staff, U.S. Air Force), "Military Assessment of Nuclear Deterrence Requirements," House Armed Services Committee, March 8, 2017, https://dod.defense.gov/Portals/1/features/2017/0917_nuclear-deterrence/docs/Transcript-HASC-Hearing-on-Nuclear-Deterrence-8-March-2017.pdf.

53 DeYoung, "Bolton and His Russian Counterpart Discuss Arms Control, Syria and Iran."

54 "Analysis of Fiscal Year 2018 National Defense Authorization Bill: HR 2810. Differences between House and Senate NDAA on Major Nuclear Provisions," Center for Arms Control and Non-Proliferation, November 2017, https://armscontrolcenter.org/wp-content/uploads/2017/11/NDAA-conference-analysis-111417.pdf.

55 The linkage of New START and INF was prompted by a speech made by President Putin in March 2018 declaring that Russia was developing new nuclear weapons systems. The House bill reiterated Secretary of Defense James Mattis's view that the systems described by Putin should comply with New START. For more on these Russian weapons, see Jeffrey Lewis, "Putin's Nuclear-Powered Cruise Missile Is Bigger than Trump's," *Foreign Policy*, March 1, 2018, https://foreignpolicy.com/2018/03/01/putins-nuclear-powered-cruise-missile-is-bigger-than-trumps/.

56 "Russia Says It Met Nuclear Limit, Questions U.S. Compliance," Voice of America, February 5, 2018, https://www.voanews.com/a/russia-nuclear-limits-us-treaty-compliance/4240224.html.

Chapter 9

1 Convention on the Prohibition of the Development, Production and Stockpiling of Bacteriological (Biological) and Toxin Weapons and on their Destruction, U.S.-U.K.-U.S.S.R., April 10, 1972, 1015 U.N.T.S. 163; and Convention on the Prohibition of the Development, Production, Stockpiling and Use of Chemical Weapons and on their Destruction, January 13, 1993, 1974 U.N.T.S. 45.

2   United Nations Office for Disarmament Affairs, Disarmament Treaties Database: Treaty on the Prohibition of Nuclear Weapons, adopted July 7, 2017, https://treaties.un.org/doc/Treaties/2017/07/20170707%2003-42%20PM/Ch_XXVI_9.pdf.

3   UN General Assembly Resolution 1(I), Establishment of a Commission to Deal with the Problems Raised by the Discovery of Atomic Energy, A/RES/1(I), ¶ 1–2(b) (January 24, 1946), http://www.un.org/en/ga/search/view_doc.asp?symbol=A/RES/1(I).

4   UN General Assembly Resolution 1(I), Establishment of a Commission, ¶ 5(c).

5   UN General Assembly Resolution 502(VI), Regulation, limitation and balanced reduction of all armed forces and all armaments; international control of atomic energy, A/RES/502(VI), ¶ 2 (January 11, 1952), http://www.un.org/en/ga/search/view_doc.asp?symbol=A/RES/502(VI).

6   Dwight D. Eisenhower, "Atoms for Peace," (speech, New York City, December 8, 1953), Dwight D. Eisenhower Presidential Library, Museum, and Childhood Home, https://www.eisenhower.archives.gov/research/online_documents/atoms_for_peace.html.

7   Eisenhower, "Atoms for Peace."

8   UN, "Atomic Energy," http://www.un.org/en/sections/issues-depth/atomic-energy/.

9   The Antarctic Treaty, December 1, 1959, 402 U.N.T.S. 71.

10 The Antarctic Treaty.

11 The Russian physicist Andrei Sakharov warned in a 1958 article that millions of people would die or suffer serious harm as a result of nuclear testing. A review of his work in 1990 concluded that his estimate—that ultimately as many as 10,000 people would suffer cancers, genetic disorders, and other ill effects for every megaton of yield in an atmospheric test—is "in good agreement with the estimate that would be made today." Andrei D. Sakharov, "Radioactive Carbon from Nuclear Explosions and Non-threshold Biological Effects," *Science & Global Security* 1 (1990): 175–87; and amended to the article, Frank von Hippel, "Appendix: Revisiting Sakharov's Assumptions," http://scienceandglobalsecurity.org/archive/sgs01sakharov.pdf.

[12] Treaty Banning Nuclear Weapon Tests in the Atmosphere, in Outer Space and Under Water (Partial Test Ban Treaty), U.S.-U.K.-U.S.S.R., August 5, 1963, 480 U.N.T.S. 43; 14 U.S.T. 1313.

[13] Treaty on the Non-Proliferation of Nuclear Weapons (NPT), U.S.-U.K.-U.S.S.R., March 5, 1970, 729 U.N.T.S. 161.

[14] Treaty on the Non-Proliferation of Nuclear Weapons, article VI.

[15] Interim Agreement between the United States of America and the Union of Soviet Socialist Republics on Certain Measures with Respect to the Limitation of Strategic Offensive Arms, U.S.-U.S.S.R., May 26, 1972; and Treaty between the United States of America and the Union of Soviet Socialist Republics on the Limitation of Anti-Ballistic Missile Systems (ABM Treaty), U.S.-U.S.S.R., May 26, 1972.

[16] The Treaty between the United States of America and the Union of Soviet Socialist Republics on Strategic Offensive Reductions (START), U.S.-U.S.S.R., July 31, 1991.

[17] The Treaty Between the United States of America and the Russian Federation on Measures for the Further Reduction and Limitation of Strategic Offensive Arms (New START), U.S.-Russian Federation, April 8, 2010.

[18] Treaty between the United States of America and the Union of Soviet Socialist Republics on the Elimination of Their Intermediate-Range and Shorter-Range Missiles (INF Treaty), U.S.-U.S.S.R., December 8, 1987.

[19] Daryl Kimball and Kingston Reif, "The Intermediate-Range Nuclear Forces (INF) Treaty at a Glance," Arms Control Association, December 2018, https://www.armscontrol.org/factsheets/INFtreaty.

[20] International Campaign to Abolish Nuclear Weapons (ICAN), www.icanw.org.

[21] Daniel M. Gerstein, "Return of Tactical Nuclear Weapons Would Send a Dangerous Signal," CNN, January 19, 2018, https://edition.cnn.com/2018/01/18/opinions/is-us-ready-for-return-of-tactical-nuclear-weapons-opinion-gerstein/index.html.

[22] UN General Assembly Resolution 71/258, Taking Forward Multilateral Nuclear Disarmament Negotiations, A/RES/71/258, ¶ 8 (December 23, 2016), http://www.un.org/en/ga/search/view_doc.asp?symbol=A/RES/71/258.

23 UN Secretary-General, "Secretary-General, in Message for Hiroshima Peace Memorial Service, Hails Dedication of Citizens to Teaching about Threat Posed by Nuclear Weapons," UN Statement SG/SM/19156-DC/3782, August 6, 2018, https://www.un.org/press/en/2018/sgsm19156.doc.htm.

24 Treaty on the Non-Proliferation of Nuclear Weapons.

25 See W. J. Hennigan, "Donald Trump Is Playing a Dangerous Game of Nuclear Poker," *Time*, February 1, 2018, http://time.com/5128394/donald-trump-nuclear-poker/.

26 Kingston Reif, "CBO: Nuclear Arsenal to Cost $1.2 Trillion," *Arms Control Today*, December 2017, https://www.armscontrol.org/act/2017-12/news/cbo-nuclear-arsenal-cost-12-trillion.

About the Contributors

Beatrice Fihn is the executive director of the International Campaign to Abolish Nuclear Weapons (ICAN). The organization won the 2017 Nobel Peace Prize for its efforts to create the Treaty on the Prohibition of Nuclear Weapons.

Matthew Fuhrmann is a professor of political science at Texas A&M University.

Todd Harrison is the director of both Defense Budget Analysis and the Aerospace Security Project at the Center for Strategic and International Studies.

Austin Long is a nuclear policy adviser in the United States Joint Staff J5. The views expressed here are his own and do not represent the views of the Joint Staff, the Department of Defense, or any other entity.

Janne E. Nolan chaired the Nuclear Security Working Group and was a faculty member at the Elliott School of International Affairs of the George Washington University. She had extensive experience in national security in government and the private sector, holding senior staff positions in the Department of State and the U.S. Senate.

Olga Oliker is the program director for Europe and Central Asia at the International Crisis Group. She has written extensively on the foreign and security policies of Russia, Ukraine, and the Central Asian and Caucasian successor states to the Soviet Union, on domestic politics in these countries, and on U.S. policy toward the region.

Todd S. Sechser is the Pamela Feinour Edmonds and Franklin S. Edmonds Jr. Discovery Professor of Politics at the University of Virginia and a senior fellow at the Miller Center of Public Affairs.

Maggie Tennis is a senior research assistant at the Brookings Institution. Previously, she was a 2018 Nuclear Scholar with the Project on Nuclear Issues at the Center for Strategic and International Studies and a 2017 Herbert Scoville Jr. Peace Fellow.

About the Editors

Caroline Dorminey is the policy director at Women's Action for New Directions (WAND) and a former policy analyst at the Cato Institute. At WAND, she manages a portfolio of nuclear policy, arms control, and defense politics issues. She is an expert with the Forum on the Arms Trade and a contributor to the Pentagon Budget Campaign.

Eric Gomez is a policy analyst in defense and foreign policy studies at the Cato Institute. His research focuses on U.S. military strategy and nuclear deterrence in East Asia. In 2018, he presented research on missile defense and U.S.-China nuclear stability at the Project on Nuclear Issues Fall Conference.

Cato Institute

Founded in 1977, the Cato Institute is a public policy research foundation dedicated to broadening the parameters of policy debate to allow consideration of more options that are consistent with the principles of limited government, individual liberty, and peace. To that end, the Institute strives to achieve greater involvement of the intelligent, concerned lay public in questions of policy and the proper role of government.

The Institute is named for *Cato's Letters*, libertarian pamphlets that were widely read in the American Colonies in the early 18th century and played a major role in laying the philosophical foundation for the American Revolution.

Despite the achievement of the nation's Founders, today virtually no aspect of life is free from government encroachment. A pervasive intolerance for individual rights is shown by government's arbitrary intrusions into private economic transactions and its disregard for civil liberties. And while freedom around the globe has notably increased in the past several decades, many countries have moved in the opposite direction, and most governments still do not respect or safeguard the wide range of civil and economic liberties.

To address those issues, the Cato Institute undertakes an extensive publications program on the complete spectrum of policy issues. Books, monographs, and shorter studies are commissioned to examine the federal budget, Social Security, regulation, military spending, international trade, and myriad other issues. Major policy conferences are held throughout the year, from which papers are published thrice yearly in the *Cato Journal*. The Institute also publishes the quarterly magazine *Regulation*.

In order to maintain its independence, the Cato Institute accepts no government funding. Contributions are received from foundations, corporations, and individuals, and other revenue is generated from the sale of publications. The Institute is a nonprofit, tax-exempt, educational foundation under Section 501(c)3 of the Internal Revenue Code.

CATO INSTITUTE
1000 Massachusetts Ave., NW
Washington, DC 20001
www.cato.org